Critical Issues in Educational Leadership ~~Series~~
Joseph Murphy, Series Editor

LEARNING TOGETHER, LEADING TOGETHER

Changing Schools through Professional Learning Communities

SHIRLEY M. HORD

Editor

Teachers College
Columbia University
New York and London

National Staff
Development Council
Oxford, Ohio

The chapters in this book are based on research and development conducted by the Southwest Educational Development Laboratory, sponsored by the U.S. Department of Education, Office of Educational Research and Improvement under contract number RJ6006081. The content herein does not necessarily reflect the views of the Department of Education, any other agency of the U.S. Government, or any other source.

Published simultaneously by Teachers College Press, 1234 Amsterdam Avenue, New York, NY 10027 and by the National Staff Development Council, P.O. Box 240, Oxford, OH 45056

Library of Congress Cataloging-in-Publication Data

Learning together, leading together : changing schools through
   professional learning communities / Shirley M. Hord, editor.
        p. cm. — (Critical issues in educational leadership series)
     Includes bibliographical references (p.) and index.
     ISBN 0-8077-4412-3 (cloth : alk. paper) — ISBN 0-8077-4411-5
     (pbk. : alk. paper)
        1. Teachers—Professional relationships.   2. School
     improvement programs.   I. Hord, Shirley M.   II. Series.
   LB1775.L37   2004
   371.1—dc22   2003060213

ISBN 0-8077-4411-5 (paper)
ISBN 0-8077-4412-3 (cloth)

Printed on acid-free paper
Manufactured in the United States of America

11   10   09   08   07   06   05   04   8   7   6   5   4   3   2   1

Contents

Acknowledgments

This manuscript has benefited enormously from the collegial participation of Leslie Blair, Southwest Education Development Laboratory communications associate, whose editorial skills and in-house production capacities contributed significantly to the clarity and readability of this document. All the authors are grateful for Leslie's support and expertise.

We also appreciate the administrators and teaching professionals in the elementary, middle, and high schools that participated in the projects from which the stories in this book came. These schools and their staffs constituted the living laboratories where we learned about the value and structure of professional learning communities, and how to initiate their development where they did not exist.

Further, we acknowledge the contributions of our co-developer colleagues whose work in schools is not reported directly in this book, but whose experiences expanded and enhanced our knowledge and understanding of how professional learning communities operate in schools for the benefit of both the staff and their students.

Dedication

This book and my work with professional learning communities would not have been possible without the experiences provided by Gene E. Hall, who directed the development of the Concerns-Based Adoption Model at The University of Texas' Research & Development Center for Teacher Education. During the course of the research and development of the Concerns-Based Adoption Model, the staff and director created a learning community where leadership, power, and authority were dispersed across the highly collegial staff. At the time, such an interactive way of working was not the norm in most organizations. This infrastructure supported the productivity of a staff who became energized and deeply committed to the work that they collaboratively designed. To Gene, these experiences were truly a gift and to him go abundant thanks and sincere gratitude.

John L. Dibert Elementary School's staff proved that the learning community concept could be established in a public elementary school. This school, on the edge of the industrial area of New Orleans, had changed itself from a highly bureaucratic and autocratically run school to one of democratic participation. This transformation was accommodated by the leadership and guidance of four successive principals: Lucianne Carmichael, Clif St. Germain, Nancy Picard, and Wiley Ates. To them, whose passion for honoring and serving children led to the creation of a professional learning community, we express our profound appreciation for our initial opportunity to learn how such a way of working in schools can benefit children.

—Shirley Hord

CHAPTER 1

Introduction

Shirley M. Hord

This book represents more than 9 years of study by professionals working for and with the Southwest Educational Development Laboratory (SEDL). It is an attempt to distill more than a decade of national attention to and conversation about school renewal and reform through the creation of professional learning communities.

In 1992, staff from SEDL were alerted to a school in our region that was markedly different in atmosphere and educational results from those around it. In that school, we found an organization that was vibrant with learning—among both students and teachers. The school staff saw themselves as a community of learners where the entire school learned together—teachers, parents, and students. They all shared a common vision of what the school should accomplish and what type of environment it should have. Teachers were innovative and encouraged to reflect on their practice. They were involved in shared decision-making. If conflict occurred it was shared openly and resolved.

At that time, we were not yet familiar with the term "professional learning communities," but we invested 4 years to follow this school's work and to learn from it. In 1995 we began to consider how to enable other schools to work as a community of learners like our model school, and launched an inquiry into what we called "communities of continuous inquiry and improvement," known in the literature as professional learning communities (PLCs). Our first task was to conduct a literature review, which informed us that there were other schools flourishing through democratic leadership and ongoing professional development, and that they were called "professional learning communities." A number of characteristics were identified with these communities; we boiled them down to five major themes: supportive and shared leadership, shared values and vision, collective learning and application of that learning, supportive conditions, and shared personal practice.

These five dimensions came to represent essential qualities and characteristics of professional learning communities. Chapter 2 discusses more fully the five dimensions. Once we identified these markers, we then set out to find more schools that shared them.

INITIATING THE WORK WITH PROFESSIONAL LEARNING COMMUNITIES

As part of SEDL's Creating Communities of Continuous Inquiry and Improvement project (CCCII), SEDL staff explored our five-state region (Arkansas, Louisiana, New Mexico, Oklahoma, Texas) from 1995 through 1997, seeking to find at least one school in each state that exhibited the five dimensions of a professional learning community. We sought to learn from principals, teachers, and others connected to these schools how they went about creating an environment that supported the five dimensions.

This first research effort is described in Chapter 3 of this book, and the results are presented in Chapters 4–6 by members of the SEDL staff. These first controlled glimpses into the PLC environment challenged some assumptions and created new understandings. They informed our next steps, and influenced our approach to further research and experimentation. They also raised important questions about leadership, democracy, and change. Shared leadership emerged as a critical component of successful professional learning communities—and yet, the level of shared leadership achieved, turned out to be almost entirely dependent upon the principal's willingness to share authority and his or her ability to motivate teachers to take on new responsibilities. We explore the irony of imposed democracy in Chapters 4 and 5, which examine the ways in which principals can act as role models of continuous learning, enhance teacher efficacy, and build trust among teachers and between teachers and administrators as their schools become professional learning communities. In Chapter 6, we discuss how leadership affects the creation and sustenance of PLCs.

THE NEXT STEP: CREATING NEW PROFESSIONAL LEARNING COMMUNITIES

Although that first phase of the CCCII project helped us better understand PLCs and the individual schools we studied, it yielded little in-depth first-hand understanding of the actions that external facilitators and the professional staff within the school took to create PLCs. SEDL staff believed that studying schools in the process of developing a community of learners was the only way to capture the details of such an endeavor. This led to the second phase of CCCII—attempting to create PLCs in diverse schools across the region.

In the fall of 1997, SEDL extended an invitation to selected colleagues within the region, and a few outside the region known to have special interest in school improvement, to become involved in a 3-year project. This project was designed to understand better how schools develop as professional learning communities. Many of those who were invited to join our study had been participants in a school leadership project developed in an earlier laboratory contract.

Thirty individuals—practitioners and consultants from higher education faculties, state education agencies, intermediate education agencies, local education agencies, a regional development laboratory, and individual school campuses—agreed to become co-developers, to work in close collaboration with SEDL in four capacities:

1. as members and collaborators in the process of developing into a professional learning community themselves,
2. as external facilitators and field-based developers to individual schools,
3. as contributors and documenters of the research effort, and
4. as disseminators of information about the PLC study to other audiences.

Eleven co-developers dropped out of the study due to illness, family circumstances, job demands, and new job assignments—all the stuff of "real life." Nineteen endured, contributing stories to the project; and insight, wisdom, and life to this book.

These co-developers entered 22 schools, most in the five-state region that SEDL serves, but also in the Northwest, Midwest, Southeast, and along the eastern seaboard of the United States. As principals, superintendents, known supporters, and total strangers, these co-developers set out to transform—and record the transformation of—ten elementary schools, eight middle/junior high schools, three high schools, and one K–8 school. They also determined to transform themselves into a professional learning community of researchers and developers. Chapters 7–13, written by the co-developers, provide a record of their preparation and journey. We also hope their accounts serve as an invitation to others to critically consider the PLC model, to imagine the ways it might be reproduced, and to pursue paths not taken or not yet completed in research and implementation.

Changing schools is highly challenging, complex, and messy work— and change is rarely welcomed. As these chapters recount, it has taken considerable time for the co-developers, relative strangers entering complex organizations, to gain knowledge and understanding of the people, policies, norms, and resources that would influence actions and outcomes for school staff. We offer these chapters as stories from some midway point—far enough along to assess the character of the journey and testify to its values.

THE CONTINUING CHALLENGE

This volume represents just the beginning of what must be an intensive and well-controlled pattern of research and measurement of professional learning communities. It seems obvious that a community of learners would inspire learning, and yet PLCs still lack the credibility that comes from substantial research reporting improved outcomes for staff and students.

Qualitative studies are dependent upon the skill, competence, and commitment of the researcher in capturing and documenting data pertinent to the inquiry. Our co-developers varied in their skills and understanding—and in their interest in recording the challenging and quite consuming activities in which they were engaged. While SEDL provided training, encouragement, and technical support in data collection processes, the underlying skills and interests of our co-developers continued to shine through. Much more research is necessary to illuminate the experience of PLCs in a greater variety of schools, and to raise the cumulative worth of these qualitative studies through the infusion of more abundant data.

Questions of leadership and implementation deserve and require further attention. The most successful PLC schools we discovered were catalyzed by an external crisis or opportunity and led by a powerful administrator who transformed the external force into energy for internal change. And yet, PLCs are essentially democratic structures. How, we wonder, does one create the collaborative, democratic, and challenging environment of a PLC without relying upon external factors or resorting to autocratic imposition of change? Assuming we find the means to nurture democracies in schools, how do we train and retrain principals, superintendents, and other district personnel to let go of the reins and allow these democracies to flourish?

There is much work still to be done in order to fully understand and successfully implement professional learning communities in schools. We hope this volume inspires our readers to join us in these efforts.

CHAPTER 2

Professional Learning Communities: An Overview

Shirley M. Hord

Significant progress has been made during this century in opening school-house doors to all, regardless of race, gender, and socioeconomic standing. We have also been in a period of unparalleled focus on accountability, standards, and comprehensive school reform. Yet a remarkable—and often disturbing—variability still exists from state to state, district to district, and school to school in the quality of educational experiences offered to children and youth. On the one hand are schools that are successfully redesigning themselves to become organizations that continually learn and invent new ways to increase the effectiveness of their work—schools that are focused on improving student learning. On the other hand are schools that have changed only minimally, applying knowledge and practices that, at best, merely maintain the status quo. Student achievement data suggest that too many schools fit into this latter category. The question of how to transform low-performing or underperforming schools into high-achieving schools is not easily answered. But as we will discuss in this book, professional learning communities can play a major role in turning troubled schools around.

A BRIEF HISTORY OF PROFESSIONAL LEARNING COMMUNITIES

The consequences of outmoded structures, practices, and relationships that exist in many of our schools have been widely publicized. In 1983, the National Commission on Excellence in Education published *A Nation at Risk*, which helped spark an ongoing national reform movement in the United States. This seminal report identified problems in the teaching profession ranging from poorly qualified teachers to poor pre-service training as contributing to a crisis in the education of children.

At about the same time, researchers began to focus on the influence of the work setting and culture on workers—in both the private corporate world and the public education sector. By the late 1980s teacher workplace factors were introduced into the discussion of teaching quality. Researcher Susan Rosenholtz (1989) found that teachers who felt *supported* in their own ongoing learning and classroom practice were more committed and effective than those who did not. Support by means of teacher networks, cooperation among colleagues, and expanded professional roles increased teacher efficacy for meeting students' needs. Further, Rosenholtz found that teachers with a strong sense of their own efficacy were more likely to adopt new classroom behaviors and that a strong sense of efficacy encouraged teachers to stay in the profession.

In 1990, Peter Senge's book *The Fifth Discipline* arrived in bookstores and began popping up in the boardrooms of corporate America. Senge suggested that performing for someone else's approval—rather than learning to become more adaptable and to generate creative solutions to problems—creates the very conditions that ensure mediocre performance. Control mechanisms paralyze both employees and leaders, allowing them only to maintain their organizations as machines. Rather than reflecting trust in those across the organization to use their creativity in order to find localized solutions to problems—solutions that are consistent with the purpose and values of the overall organization—solutions are mandated that are poorly suited to the real problem at hand.

Senge advocated, instead, a different organizational structure, better suited to our complex, interdependent, and fast-changing society. Such an organization is oriented toward *learning* rather than controlling mechanisms. Senge saw this newly conceptualized learning organization as one "where people continually expand their capacity to create the results they truly desire, where new and expansive patterns of thinking are nurtured, where collective aspiration is set free, and where people are continually learning how to learn together" (Senge, 1990, p. 3).

Over the next year or so, Senge's book and his description of *learning organizations* moved into the educational environment. As Senge's paradigm was explored by educators and shared in educational journals, the label became *learning communities*.

McLaughlin and Talbert (1993) seemed to support this fledgling educational paradigm as they confirmed Rosenholtz's findings, suggesting that when teachers had opportunities for collaborative inquiry and its related learning, the result was a body of wisdom about teaching that could be widely shared. Shared decision-making became widely discussed as a factor related to curriculum reform and in the transformation of teaching roles in some schools (Darling-Hammond, 1996). In such schools, structured time was provided for teachers to work together in planning instruction, observing each other's classrooms, and sharing feedback. Researchers also began observing improvements in schools where the faculty was functioning as a learning community (Brandt, 1996; Lee, Smith, & Croninger, 1995; Newmann & Wehlage, 1995; Scribner & Reyes, 1999).

During this same time, SEDL's work on PLCs was evolving. We had visited and studied John Dibert Elementary School, a school that had not only remained a learning community through a succession of four principals, but had become a stronger learning community during that time. We also undertook the Creating Communities of Continuous Inquiry and Improvement (CCCII) project as a way to learn more about how to nurture learning communities in schools across the SEDL region.

CHARACTERISTICS OF PROFESSIONAL LEARNING COMMUNITIES

The literature is quite clear about the characteristics of academically successful professional learning communities. At the beginning of the CCCII project, we organized the characteristics of PLCs into five themes or dimensions:

- *Supportive and shared leadership* requires the collegial and facilitative participation of the principal who shares leadership—and thus, power and authority—by inviting staff input and action in decision-making.
- *Shared values and vision* include an unwavering commitment to student learning that is consistently articulated and referenced in the staff's work.
- *Collective learning and application of learning* requires that school staff at all levels are engaged in processes that collectively seek new knowledge among staff and application of the learning to solutions that address students' needs.
- *Supportive conditions* include physical conditions and human capacities that encourage and sustain a collegial atmosphere and collective learning.
- *Shared practice* involves the review of a teacher's behavior by colleagues and includes feedback and assistance activity to support individual and community improvement.

These dimensions are not isolated, but are intertwined. Each dimension affects the others in a variety of ways.

Supportive and Shared Leadership

It seems clear—if also somewhat ironic—that transforming the school organization into a learning community can be done only with the leaders' sanction and active nurturing of the entire staff's development as a community. Lucianne Carmichael (1982), first resident principal of the Harvard University Principal Center and a principal who nurtured a professional community of learners at Dibert Elementary, discussed the authority and power position held when a principal is viewed as all-wise and all-competent by the staff who are on the lower rungs of the power-structure ladder. Such a principal enjoys—or is entrapped by—a sense of "omnicompetence," internalized by the principal and reinforced by others in schools, which makes it difficult to admit to any need for professional development or to recognize the dynamic potential of staff contributions to decision-making. Furthermore, it is difficult for most staff to propose divergent views or ideas about the school's effectiveness when the principal is seen in such a dominant position.

Carmichael proposed that the notion of principals' omnicompetence be "ditched" in favor of principals' participation in professional development. Administrators, along with teachers, must be learners: questioning, investigating, and seeking solutions for school improvement and increased student achievement. The traditional pattern that "teachers teach, students learn and administrators manage is completely altered. ... [There is] no longer a hierarchy of who knows more than someone else, but rather the need for everyone to contribute" (Kleine-Kracht, 1993, p. 393). As we will see in later chapters, to foster shared leadership, the principal must encourage others to assume leadership roles and be able to recognize when staff, parents, or others are ready to take on leadership roles.

One of the principals at Dibert who succeeded Carmichael shared these reflections:

> The two principals who preceded me had a real commitment to share decision-making and move teachers toward ownership in what was going on in the school, so when I came it was clearly understood when I interviewed for the position that was the way we did business. ... If you are not intimidated by that, then you put your faith in the people you work with ... and get a great deal accomplished. (Boyd & Hord, 1994a, pp. 19–20)

Shared Values and Vision

A shared vision is a particular mental image of what is important to an individual and to an organization; it is a preferred image of the future that compels staff to work toward that image. A core characteristic of the professional learning community is an undeviating focus on student learning (Louis & Kruse, 1995). In the PLC vision then, students are pictured as academically capable and staff envision learning environments to support and realize each student's potential achievement.

Staff are encouraged not only to be involved in the process of developing a shared vision, but to use that vision as a guide in making all decisions about teaching and learning in the school. The values and goals expressed in the vision will determine how staff members spend their time, what problems they solve, and how resources are distributed.

Once the vision has been agreed upon, it is the principal's role to keep reminding stakeholders of the vision. School leaders must communicate and articulate forceful images of what an organization wants to create, sharing pictures of the future that foster genuine commitment. Throughout the school year and around the school building there should be continual reminders of the vision—of the high levels of student achievement and learning that the school is working toward.

In a PLC, the individual staff member is responsible for his or her actions, but due to shared vision and values, the common good is placed on a par with personal ambition. When a school creates such a community, individual talent and commitment are harnessed into a group effort that pushes for high-quality learning for all students (Brandt, 1995).

Collective Learning and Its Application

The professional learning community in schools is demonstrated by staff from multiple grade levels and departments at all levels, collaboratively and continually learning and working together. Such collaborative work is grounded in *reflective dialogue* or *inquiry*, where staff conduct conversations about students and teaching and learning, identifying related issues and problems.

Participants in these reflection and learning conversations apply new ideas and information to problem solving and are therefore able to create new conditions for students, whether it is through establishing a new curriculum, revising instruction practices, or stepping up instruction and expectations. The key to the importance of this inquiry is that it is a continuous, ongoing process that focuses on students and their benefits. Collective inquiry and learning allows staff to develop in ways that can produce the kinds of changes necessary for increased student learning and school improvement. Staff spend time assessing whether they have been effective and decide what they need to learn to become more effective in their efforts to help students become successful learners. They then learn the skills and strategies they have deemed necessary, apply these skills and strategies, and monitor progress in using these skills.

Supportive Conditions

Supportive conditions determine *when, where,* and *how* the staff regularly come together as a unit to do the learning, decision-making, problem solving, and creative work that characterize a professional learning community. For learning communities to function productively, supportive conditions include the physical or structural conditions that enable shared leadership, collective learning, and shared practice. They also include certain capacities of the people involved in the learning community.

Physical and Structural Factors. The following physical factors that support learning communities have been identified: time to meet and talk, small size of the school and physical proximity of the staff to one another, teaching roles that are interdependent, communication structures, school autonomy, and teacher empowerment (Louis & Kruse, 1995). Boyd's (1992) list of physical factors in a context conducive to school change and improvement is similar: the availability of resources; schedules and structures that reduce isolation; and policies that provide greater autonomy, foster collaboration, provide effective communication, and provide for staff development.

It is no surprise that time is a significant issue for faculties that wish to work together collegially. It has been cited as both a barrier (when it is not available) and a supportive factor (when it is present) by staffs engaging in school improvement. Compounding the problem is that time needed for working together may conflict with district rules and regulations, parent and educator expectations, and collective bargaining agreements. In our work at SEDL, we have found schools must be creative when it comes to allocating time. For example, at Dibert Elementary, 4 days a week the staff adopted a longer school day in order to release students early on Thursdays. On these early release Thursdays, the faculty engaged in Faculty Study—the staff's time to meet for collective inquiry and learning.

Regarding the factor of small size of the school, it may be necessary in large schools for faculty to form smaller groups to meet for collective learning. We have found, however, that faculties as large as 30–40 members can easily work together in one group.

Human Capacities. Individuals in a productive learning community must be willing to accept feedback and work toward improvement (Louis & Kruse, 1995). In addition, there should be respect and trust among colleagues at the school and district level, supportive leadership from administrators and others in key roles, and relatively intensive socialization processes. Faculty should possess an appropriate cognitive and skill base that enables effective teaching and learning as well.

Note the strong parallel with people or human factors identified by Boyd (1992) as necessary for school change: positive teachers' attitudes toward schooling, students, and change; students' heightened interest in and engagement with learning (this may be construed as both an outcome and an input, it seems); norms of continuous critical inquiry and continuous improvement; widely shared vision or sense of purpose; norm of involvement in decision-making; collegial relationships among teachers; positive, caring student-teacher-administrator relationships; and a sense of community in the school. Boyd also noted two factors beyond the school staff that can enhance a PLC: supportive community attitudes and parents and community members as partners and allies. Principals can nurture the human capacities needed for PLCs by helping staff relate to each other, providing some social activities for staff members to get to know each other on a personal level, and creating a caring environment.

Shared Personal Practice

Just as most school reform efforts are likely to provide appropriate learning environments for students, we should provide such an environment for teachers as well. Teachers, too, need "an environment that values and supports hard work, the acceptance of challenging tasks, risk taking, and the promotion of growth" (Midgley & Wood, 1993, p. 252). Shared personal practice contributes to such a setting.

In PLCs, review of a teacher's practice and behavior by colleagues should be the norm. The practice is not an evaluative process, but part of the "peers helping peers" process that includes teachers visiting each other's classrooms on a regular basis to observe, take notes, and discuss their observations with the teacher they have visited. In the process, teachers act as change facilitators for each other, supporting the adoption of new practices through peer coaching and feedback. The process is based on the desire for individual and community improvement and is enabled by the mutual respect and trust among staff members. Because of the amount of trust involved and the history of isolation most teachers have experienced, this is often the last dimension of a PLC to develop.

Wignall (1992) describes a high school in which teachers share their practice and enjoy a high level of collaboration in their daily work life. Mutual respect and understanding are the fundamental requirements for this kind of workplace culture. Teachers find help, support, and trust as a result of the development of warm relationships with one another.

"Teachers tolerate (even encourage) debate, discussion and disagreement. They are comfortable sharing both their successes and their failures. They praise and recognize one another's triumphs, and offer empathy and support for each other's troubles" (p. 18).

OUTCOMES OF PROFESSIONAL LEARNING COMMUNITIES FOR STAFF AND STUDENTS

Research provides strong evidence that low-performing schools can overcome barriers and challenges that accompany reform efforts and increase student achievement when the staff and school are organized as a professional learning community.

The Center on Organization and Restructuring of Schools published findings on 11,000 students enrolled in 820 secondary schools across the nation (Lee, Smith, & Croninger, 1995). In the schools that were characterized by professional learning communities, the staff had worked together and changed their classroom pedagogy. As a result, they engaged students in high intellectual learning tasks, and students achieved greater academic gains in math, science, history, and reading than students in traditionally organized schools. In addition, the achievement gaps between students from different backgrounds were smaller in those schools, students learned more and, in the smaller high schools, learning was distributed more equitably.

The schools in the study were communally organized and promoted a setting in which staff (and students) were committed to the mission of the school and worked together to strengthen that mission. Staff members saw themselves as responsible for the total development of the students and shared collective responsibility for the success of students. In such schools, "teachers and other staff members experience more satisfaction and higher morale, while students drop out less often and cut fewer classes. And both staff and students post lower rates of absenteeism" (Lee, Smith, & Croninger, 1995, p. 5).

The work of the Center on Organization and Restructuring of Schools (Newmann & Wehlage, 1995) comprises four complementary studies including rigorous 3- and 4-year longitudinal case-study approaches, as well as survey methods and collection of student test data. Data cover 1,500 elementary, middle, and high schools throughout the United States, with field research in 44 schools in 16 states. The result showed that comprehensive redesign of schools, including decentralization, shared decision-making, schools within schools, teachers teaming, and/or professional communities of staff, can improve student learning. Four interconnected factors leading to improved student outcomes were identified. These four factors are also supported by professional learning communities and are likely to be present when a school develops a PLC.

1. *Student learning.* Teachers agree on a vision of authentic (in agreement with real-world experience or actuality, not contrived) and high-quality intellectual work for students that includes intellectually challenging learning tasks and clear goals for high-quality learning. This vision is communicated to students and parents.
2. *Authentic pedagogy.* High-quality student learning is achieved in classrooms through authentic pedagogy (instruction and assessment), and students of all social backgrounds benefit equally, regardless of race, gender, or family income.
3. *Organizational capacity.* In order to provide learning of high intellectual quality, the capacity of the staff to work well as a unit must be developed. The most successful schools functioned as professional communities, where teachers helped one another, took collective (not just individual) responsibility for student learning, and worked continuously to improve their teaching practices. Schools with strong professional communities offered more authentic pedagogy and were more effective in encouraging student achievement.
4. *External support.* Schools need essential financial, technical, and political support from districts, state and federal agencies, parents, and other citizens.

SEDL's work with low-performing schools has indicated there are distinct parallels between issues with which low-performing schools struggle and the five dimensions that support PLCs in higher-performing schools (Morrissey, 2000). For example, low-performing schools often lack the organizational supports that PLCs require and that enable schools to run efficiently and effectively. Low-performing schools may not have the structures for strong communication among school staff, district staff, parents, and community members that are usually apparent in PLC schools. There may be no processes in place for problem solving or collaboration. Likewise, at low-performing schools, a staff-wide understanding and focus on improvement strategies is often lacking and there is little support for teachers to learn new practices.

Evidence exists that schools in which teachers act in collaborative settings to deeply examine teaching and learning, and then discuss effective instructional practices, show academic results for students more quickly than schools that do not (Darling-Hammond, 1995). Such an environment also helps secondary-level teachers increase their understanding of the content they teach and the roles they play. This increased understanding contributes to improved instruction that helps all children achieve expectations (McLaughlin & Talbert, 1993).

There is, of course, no certainty that organizing staffs into learning communities will eliminate all of the problems facing low-performing schools. But it seems quite plausible that the opportunities provided by regular meetings of learning communities, their inquiry into innovative solutions to student learning, and the thoughtful examination of new programs and practices will result in the kind of understanding and learning needed to implement and sustain school improvement strategies. The PLC is not an improvement program or plan, but it provides a structure for schools to continuously improve by building staff capacity for learning and change.

If strong results such as those mentioned above are linked to teachers and administrators working in professional learning communities, how might the frequency of such communities in schools be increased? The remaining chapters in this book provide insights into how to develop conditions necessary for PLCs. Widespread development of PLCs cannot occur, however, without a paradigm shift, among the public, and among educators themselves about what the role of the teacher entails. Many in the public, and in the profession believe that the only legitimate use of a teacher's time is standing in front of the class, working directly with students. In studies comparing how teachers around the world spend their time, it is clear that in countries such as Japan, teachers teach fewer classes, using a greater portion of their time in planning, conferring with colleagues, working with students individually, visiting other classrooms, and engaging in other professional development activities (Darling-Hammond, 1994, 1996). Changing perspectives to enable the public and the profession to understand and value teacher professional development will require focused and concerted effort.

Lucianne Carmichael has said, "Teachers are the first learners." Through their participation in a professional learning community, teachers become the first learners, continuous learners, and more effective teachers. In turn, student outcomes increase—a goal upon which we can all agree.

CHAPTER 3

Study Description:
Investigating Five PLC Schools

D'Ette Cowan, Grace L. Fleming,
Tara Leo Thompson, and Melanie S. Morrissey

As mentioned in Chapter 1, SEDL's initial research project for Creating Communities of Continuous Inquiry and Improvement (CCCII) involved studying schools that were already professional learning communities. We used the five dimensions to find schools that had become professional learning communities. It should be noted that each of these dimensions exists as a continuum bounded by exemplary PLC practices on one side and antithetical practices on the other. Schools that exhibit all characteristics at either end of the continuum are rare. We were interested in schools that appeared to be much closer to the exemplary PLC practices than the other end of the continuum.

We were also interested in studying schools that differed from one another regarding their demographic descriptions. Thus, we wanted to study PLCs that existed in a variety of settings—urban, suburban, and rural. Additionally, we wanted to include schools that had varied student ethnicity and socioeconomic status.

We used a network of key educators in SEDL's region to first identify schools that approximated professional learning communities. Very few schools that were nominated appeared to have actually created PLCs among their staffs. Principals and/or administrators in the superintendents' offices were contacted regarding the schools that appeared to be authentic candidates. From these conversations, we gained additional information to determine whether the school staffs did indeed work as PLCs and whether they were amenable to participating in the study. After considerable searching, we did find five PLCs.

The five schools, to a significant extent, represented the diversity of SEDL's region. The schools were either elementary or middle schools and varied in terms of setting, percentage of economically disadvantaged students, and number of students enrolled, as shown in Table 3.1 (pseudo-

Table 3.1. Description of Five Study Sites

	Cottonwood Creek	Bayou Bend	Violet Canyon	Green Valley	Rolling Hills
Community setting	Urban	Rural	Suburban	Urban	Suburban
Grade levels	PK–5	3–5	PK–6	7–8	PK–5
Number of students	500	370	850	340	400
Economically disadvantaged	97%	69%	46%	60%	46%

nyms are used for the names of the schools). Table 3.2 shows student ethnicity for each of the schools. Four of the schools had a predominant ethnic group—either African American, Euro American, or Hispanic. The fifth school was a nearly even mix of Euro American and Hispanic students.

DATA COLLECTION

We used two methods to engage school staffs in the study: a paper/ pencil questionnaire and one-to-one interviews.

Questionnaire

Staff members at the five schools were asked to complete a written survey, *School Professional Staff as a Learning Community* (Hord, 1996). The questionnaire is composed of 17 descriptors encompassing the five PLC dimen-

Table 3.2. Ethnic Makeup of the Student Bodies

Ethnicity	Cottonwood Creek	Bayou Bend	Violet Canyon	Green Valley	Rolling Hills
African American	5%	11%	1%	63%	5%
Euro American	10%	89%	52%	35%	80%
Hispanic	84%	0	47%	1%	6%
Native American	0	0	0	0	8%
Other	1%	0	0	1%	1%

sions. Each descriptor is further arrayed along a five-point continuum to allow the respondent to rate the degree to which the staff as a whole reflects PLC qualities. For each item, three statements describe points on the continuum representing exemplary practice, midpoint practice, and antithetical practice.

- *Exemplary practice:* The entire staff discusses visions for improvement such that consensus and a shared vision result.
- *Midpoint practice:* Visions for improvement are not thoroughly explored; some staff members agree and others do not.
- *Antithetical practice:* Visions for improvement held by the staff are widely divergent.

We mailed copies of the questionnaire to the school and asked all professional staff members to complete it individually. We used envelopes in which completed questionnaires could be sealed when they were turned in to the school office or mailed to SEDL, in order to ensure confidentiality of responses. Nearly 100% of those instruments were returned, either during a later interview visit or by mail.

Interviews

A second strategy for collecting data was through interviews. Principals, teachers, and other campus-based professional staff (e.g., counselors and librarians) were interviewed at all sites. Assistant principals, central office staff, paraprofessionals, and parents were interviewed as warranted based on pre-site visit information. We requested that the principals at each site select staff members for participation based on length of time at the school. Generally this included most staff members who had been at the school 3 to 5 years before the study. This condition was necessary to ensure feedback from individuals who had participated in the effort to change the schools' operation. The number of interviews at each school ranged from 23 to 33, for a total of 139 interviews at all five schools.

As with the questionnaire, the interviews were designed to incorporate questions pertaining to the five dimensions of a PLC. The protocol used in the interviews had broad questions designed to elicit information regarding the way the school operated in relation to each dimension of a PLC. Each of these had a series of prompting questions designed to gain more detailed information if interviewees did not supply it in their initial responses. The protocol served as a guide rather than a regimen for gaining interviewees' perspectives of their schools' professional norms and systems of operations. While the intent of the PLC instrument was to determine a school's placement, overall, on the PLC continuum, the interview protocol intended to reveal how the school came to adopt the practices related to the five dimensions.

Each interview with teachers, counselors, librarians, coaches, school support staff, and parents lasted 45 minutes in length. Interviews with administrators lasted approximately 60 to 90 minutes. At each school, all interviews were conducted with a 36-hour period. All were conducted in a private setting and were audiotaped.

DATA ANALYSIS

The interviews provided rich sources of data with more than 100 hours of discussion between interviewers and professional staff captured on tape. The tapes were transcribed in entirety following our return to SEDL. We applied a constant comparative method to sort the data according to the five dimensions of professional learning community practices. A sixth category held background information, offered by the professional staff about the school, and a seventh category held data that did not apply to the five dimensions.

The answers to each question asked by the interviewers were categorized independently even though the questions tended to be along the lines of the five dimensions. This was necessary because the information in the answers often shed light on more than one dimension or referred more directly to a dimension other than the one that shaped the question being asked. This tendency for information to bleed from one category to another required careful attention to ensure consistency within the analysis.

The data were triangulated by purposefully seeking instances of similar input from more than one interviewee. We were also attentive to instances in which disagreement existed among interviewee accounts.

Once data had been analyzed, we prepared briefing papers that presented findings in narrative format. We then submitted drafts of the briefing papers to the principals and assistant principals as a member-checking strategy for confirming the discussion points and conclusions. This review allowed school personnel to add missing pieces of data and to clarify any misunderstandings. Once revisions based on this feedback were incorporated into the papers, SEDL provided sufficient copies to the school for all the staff to review.

With the data reconfigured according to the five dimensions and a background information category, we synthesized and then examined the data for their relevance to understanding how professional learning communities can be built. The new knowledge that emerged from each school and from the schools as a group is provided in Chapters 4–6, which follow. In these chapters, readers will see how intertwined the five dimensions become and how each dimension enhances and supports the others. We will also see the critical roles the principal played at each of the five schools in developing a learning community.

CHAPTER 4

Principals and Teachers as Continuous Learners

Grace L. Fleming

In professional learning communities, teachers and administrators are actively involved in a process of continuous learning. They are active in their own learning and are open to new ideas. Collectively they seek new knowledge and ways of applying that knowledge to their work. They gather information, make decisions, and implement those decisions—cooperatively. When they have examined the options and determined the best course of action, they take measured risks in the implementation of their decisions. They monitor their progress, too, perhaps refining instruction or processes in place at school to best meet the needs of their students.

THE PRINCIPAL IS KEY TO A PLC

In our research at five schools that successfully operate as PLCs, we found clear evidence that the administrator is key to the existence of a professional learning community. So we began asking, how do principals operate in their roles to develop settings where all professional staff members take responsibility for the highest-quality learning possible at the school?

In all of the schools we examined, some external force or event provided an opening for profound change. In one, the principal took advantage of a crisis to mobilize the staff and engage them in collegial problem solving so that they explored and learned about solutions for the problems. In another, the principal seized an opportunity to develop a learning community among her staff to study the possibilities and advantages of implementing a new curriculum that was being offered to the school. Two schools faced structural challenges and opportunities when they were administratively redesigned—one broke from its district, another was formed when one large school was divided into two. In the three schools that are the focus of this chapter, the principals were continuous learners. Their ongoing personal and professional development activities informed their responses to change and allowed them to transfer their continuous learning practices to their staffs in order to create a community of professional learners.

These three principals devoted attention to their own development and were quite visible to their staffs as learners. They made sure not only that the staff knew of their efforts to keep informed, but also that the staff experienced application of their learning. One teacher described her principal's professional strengths and personal practices and the ways that these attributes benefited the school as follows:

> Professional staff development is definitely one of the strengths of our principal. She reads incessantly. She goes to workshops. She knows incredible people all over the country. She just has re-sources at her fingertips that I think a lot of people don't have. And so she brings in a lot of people and she has changed the school to a more school-wide focus.

Barbara MacNamara

Barbara MacNamara (pseudonyms are used for the names of principals and schools) had been serving at her school for 7 years when one of SEDL's researchers came to visit. The researcher was waiting for Barbara in her office and noticed a current and well-used copy of *Educational Evaluation and Policy Analysis*. The book was tagged throughout with yellow sticky notes; its pages were battered and dog-eared. Barbara seemed to be not only reading it, but studying it and using it as a reference. Teachers at her school associated Barbara with constant reading and attending conferences. "Anytime we go to her with an idea," one teacher said, "she knows what we are talking about. She has read about it or heard about it or worked with it."

Within 3 years of beginning to teach, Barbara had earned a master's of education in administration. After 10 years of teaching, she took a 2-year break to pursue a Ph.D. During that time she worked as a graduate research assistant, and was invited to participate in the development of her state's new teacher appraisal system. Later she took a one-semester sabbatical from being principal to focus again on her Ph.D. studies.

Linda Aiken

Also viewed by her staff as an administrator continuously engaged in reading and workshops for the purposes of her own learning, Linda Aiken was described by one of her teachers as always willing to learn new things. She is always sharing ideas with us of what she's learned. She herself is going to workshops and things like that. She's a member of several councils. She's involved in the PTA whereas before the administrators were never involved in that kind of stuff that goes on in the school.

Linda had a reputation for being extremely effective in networking for her own professional development and to access resources for her school. In addition to her 14 years of teaching at the elementary level and 7 years as a principal, her professional experiences included membership on various district-level committees, supervision of elementary student teachers, and numerous workshop presentations. She had a long list of trainings and workshops in which she had participated as part of her commitment to her own professional growth.

Patricia Sommers

The constant learning that Patricia Sommers had demanded of herself served her well when the school district decided to reorganize a junior high school into a middle school. Patricia spent 7 years as principal of that middle school and developed the staff as a professional learning community. One staff member said, "The middle school concept was there. And she's sharp and knew what was out there. She knew what was cutting-edge."

Patricia served in six professional positions during her 25 years in education: as teacher, assistant principal, principal, counselor, supervisor of secondary instruction, and supervisor of middle-level education. While a principal, she worked with the Middle Grades School State Policy Initiative sponsored by the Carnegie Foundation. She maintained a network of colleagues across her state and involved herself both in learning from these people and with them. She continued to conduct professional development workshops on leadership, school improvement, and school-based management in addition to participating in the design of certification programs to meet the new middle-level education professional standards for her state.

Each of these principals had been recognized by others for her leadership. Each made good use of her contacts beyond her immediate professional circle—and university, district, and state leaders called on these women for participation on committees and task forces and other projects before, during, and after their success in PLC development. Each woman remained active in such "outside" endeavors: Barbara taught graduate courses, Linda actively served on several committees, and Patricia conducted leadership training throughout her state. Their experiences contributed to their PLC work.

Their professional experiences may be responsible for another common trait these leaders held: They had a realistic understanding of change as a process that requires an ongoing commitment that oftentimes simply reduces to perseverance. The teachers in the schools where these principals worked were normal human beings who would resist change, be confused about their direction, question the sanity of their leader, and at times even openly defy the leadership that made them uncomfortable. In order for them to move from old ways of functioning to operating as a professional learning community, the principal had to constantly nurture those who understood the value of becoming a PLC and persuade those who had yet to recognize the strength of a PLC. Each of these principals dealt with friction and tension, particularly in the early stages of development.

These principals continuously scanned the horizon for new information to improve learning and achieve student success at their schools. This information was then applied at their schools, where these principals overtly modeled learning and its application. In so doing, each principal left her imprint upon her staff. Each woman turned her own ongoing learning into capacity building among the staff of her respective school. Each staff used its increased skills to improve learning conditions for students at the schools and to support their principal's continued ability to find and utilize new opportunities for learning and growth.

PRINCIPALS' STRATEGIES FOR INCREASING STAFF CAPACITIES FOR CONTINUOUS LEARNING

In order to increase staff capacities for continuous learning, these three principals used similar strategies: developing collegial relationships with staff, focusing staff on student success, making opportunities for teachers to learn, inviting teachers into decision-making and implementation, and nurturing new ways of operating. Each strategy required patience and diligence on the part of the principal while teachers figured out the new expectations and came to realize the significance of their new role in helping students learn. These principals also had the wisdom to allow the teachers time and space for adopting new behaviors and sometimes took assertive steps that made the teachers uncomfortable until they understood the value of the changes. We will discuss each strategy below.

Developing Collegial Relationships with Staff

Rather than simply filling the roles of subordinates and supervisor, the staff members of the three schools of this study benefited from close professional interactions with their principals as co-professionals. As one teacher put it, "I don't work under the principal; I work with her." Linda, Barbara, and Patricia invested the time and energy necessary for teachers to understand that collegial relationships between principals and teachers are possible and productive. Barbara shared journal articles and other sources of information with her staff members, treating them as she would her graduate school classmates. Patricia's philosophy was to always work on "both the task side and the people side" of any staff undertaking. "You've got to have both," she said, "because it's kind of like a railroad track. If you get too far down just one side, the train's going to derail."

The notion of collegiality between teacher and principal generally causes uncertainty among teachers because they naturally think in terms of hierarchy. As with many supervisor-employee relationships, the teachers expect to carry out decisions made above them in the organizational structure rather than to be part of making those decisions. To enter into a mutual relationship with the principal, they must let go of such former habits as criticizing the principal with other teachers and instead learn to openly discuss questions and concerns in the presence of the principal. An interesting note here is that the strongest advocates for these principals at the time of this research included teachers who actively resisted and criticized the principals during the earliest steps of PLC formation.

The principals knew that the most effective way to establish collegiality was to serve alongside teachers without "pulling rank" in order for their individual views to prevail in a group. At times they would put aside their own preferences to agree with the larger group's consensus for action. Each teacher interviewed had stories of his or her principal's efforts to interact personally with each teacher to learn more about the teacher's philosophy, concerns, and interests regarding teaching and learning. The teachers in Linda's and Patricia's schools reported that their principal would be supportive and help them correct any mistakes they might make. This led the teachers to their articulated belief that their principal trusted and respected them as professionals.

Focusing Staff on Student Success

Within their schools, the principals led their teachers to work and learn with a common purpose. Barbara's school had become so successful with its focus on students that real estate agents in the community could rent or sell properties near the school based on its reputation for student achievement. At Linda's school, every member of the staff identified the vision for students and the school, and they were clear on their roles in working to make that vision a reality. Patricia's teachers often mentioned what they called the *first filter*: "If it's good for kids, it's possible. If it's not good for kids, we don't need to do it." But they did not start with this attitude. Again, because of the traditional view of organizational hierarchy, teachers felt an obligation to answer to those above them in the system, such as principals and superintendents. By focusing on student success, they had to learn to become advocates for what they believed children needed most in their schools. The teachers learned this advocacy role by following their principal's lead, and by the time they had formed their PLC they naturally demonstrated values that concerned students and student success.

Making Opportunities for Teachers to Learn

The principals structured gatherings for group learning that involved the whole staff. Barbara set aside a half day each month for an all-staff Faculty Study. Linda's teachers knew that she directed as much money as possible to staff development. While these efforts took different forms at each school, the intent was the same: involve the teachers in learning more and sharing that new knowledge with each other.

The teachers at all three schools developed group learning practices that included research, synthesis, and discussion of information on topics related to school operations and instruction. These practices were common at staff meetings, study groups, and committee operations. According to the teachers at Patricia's school, if they walked into a room and saw multiple chart pads on easels, they automatically divided themselves into groups that included both genders, all races, and each grade level.

Teachers at these three schools knew that their participation in conferences and workshops off-campus included responsibility to bring back information and actively share it with their colleagues. This sharing often included formally structured presentations to and discussions with the staff, as well as informal information exchanges in between classes and in the teachers' lounge. The genuine enthusiasm for learning was palpable at these schools. The principals nurtured staff enthusiasm by modeling their own learning and providing opportunities for all staff to learn.

Inviting Teachers into Decision-Making and Implementation

Each principal developed her own organizational structure to incorporate and support staff involvement in decisions for the school. Barbara consulted with teachers individually or in small groups about decisions pertinent to them, such as schedules for and departmentalization of the school. Linda developed a two-tiered system for including teachers in decision-making. Teachers participated in design teams focused on specific issues.

The chair of each design team represented that team in the School Leadership Council, where decisions were made to guide the development and implementation of the school's priorities. Each spring term, the staff at Patricia's school chose a theme for the following school year, which then guided the staff teams that determined curriculum and instruction for that year.

To make these strategies work, the principal sometimes agreed to accept a staff or committee decision that was different from what she would have chosen herself. Thus, it is clear that principals involved in PLC development must have healthy egos, nurtured by operating within a professional learning community rather than taking credit for individual decisions. By sharing responsibility and credit for decision-making, Barbara, Linda, and Patricia were consistently rewarded with good results. Not only were these staff and committee decisions effective; the staff members involved were encouraged to invest further in their school. This strategy increased both the capacity and the commitment of staff for taking responsibility for their schools.

Nurturing New Ways of Operating

Each of our three principals made concerted efforts to create conditions at their individual schools that were optimal for teachers to adapt to new ways of working in the school. These efforts included both organizational structures and human relationships. Each principal used her creativity to change the school schedules and arrange time for whole staff planning and meeting. These women also prepared their teachers to make good use of this time. In addition, Barbara developed a "buddy system," which paired teachers who worked with the same students as a means of mutual support. Linda moved the Special Education Department at her school from an isolated area of campus into the main building of the school. This change increased the amount of interaction between Special Education teachers and all other teachers. Patricia also rearranged her school by placing same-grade-level classes in the same hallway to increase teacher collegiality and support between classes and during breaks.

Linda and Patricia found that these decisions to rearrange the school in terms of which teachers were assigned to which classrooms disconcerted many teachers. They were met with the chorus, "We've never done it that way before." However, both women had the patience to support their teachers while they adjusted to the changes and to guide their behaviors while they learned to make good use of the new configurations. In both cases, the teachers ultimately understood the importance of proximity to their peers once they mastered the other PLC strategies for work-ing and learning together.

The building of relationships was continuous and reinforced other strategies. At each school, the principal initiated relationship building by modeling with all teachers individually what it meant to trust, support, and encourage others. As teachers began to support one another, the fear of failure gave way to a concern for finding effective strategies for improving teaching and learning. One teacher explained,

> The principal strongly encourages the teachers to identify and try
> new things that they feel might be beneficial to students. When
> she does this, the teachers feel no threat of failing, for the principal
> gives them full support under any conditions.

Staff relationships were also nurtured through communication meth-ods ranging from newsletters to daily announcements to lunchroom shar-ing. As the PLCs developed, staff increasingly took responsibility for strengthening their relationships with their colleagues.

TEACHERS RESPOND TO PRINCIPALS' MODELS

The teachers at the three schools increasingly emulated the examples set by their principals. The principals demonstrated the meaning of a professional learning community by sharing their own learning with their staffs and orchestrating opportunities for their staffs to incorporate those same practices. These principals valued the expertise that their teachers possessed and were able to tap it. Staff responded as professionals and willingly expanded their understanding of their personal responsibility as teachers. In the process, these teachers came to value the PLC itself, as it increased their effectiveness and tapped into their creativity. We see this teacher regard for the PLC in the practices they initiated indepen-dently. These practices reflected certain themes that surfaced across all three schools, and are discussed below.

Looking for Ways to Improve Learning Conditions for Students

Just like their principals, these teachers were constantly learning about their profession. Some were reading; others were attending workshops and conferences. All assumed that whatever they learned must be brought back to their colleagues at their schools. When one school identified literacy as a major concern for their students, 34 teachers joined a literacy instruction class that met once a week for 2 hours after school. Their plan? One of the teachers explained, "What we are trying to do is start the small-core group on implementing this, and then next year open it up. The teachers who are being trained will train the other teachers."

Trusting Colleagues

The importance of relationships was clear in these schools. Teachers willingly put energy into their relationships with each other, including the time to know about one another's personal lives. Caring about one another translated into trusting each other professionally, which was critical to being able to work together as a whole staff. In one case, the art teacher had been alienated by a previous principal and staff were ineffective at including her in their activities due to rising ill feelings. When Patricia became their principal and began developing a PLC, the teachers then had permission to actively reach out to the art teacher, who in turn became a key figure in school morale by revamping the school entrance with trophy cases that held art work and various symbols of their community and their school in addition to the athletic trophies from years gone by. This teacher also began to offer assistance and festive creativity anytime the school planned special events or celebrations. The teacher soon became one of the individuals in that school and all of the PLC schools who expressed confidence that action taken and decisions made by committees would be in the best interest of the school as a whole.

Asking Other Teachers for Advice

Teachers at the three schools recognized other teachers for their expertise and actively sought counsel regarding particular students and classroom management as well as instruction. They readily exchanged information with each other and encouraged one another in their professional practice. Linda's school staff organized themselves into Critical Friends groups, as proposed by the Annenberg Institute. Teachers were beginning to look at instructional plans, assignments, and student products, and then arrange to visit classrooms in order to observe instruction. "The Critical Friends movement is going to help us," asserted one teacher, "and give us more opportunity to really discuss student work to begin with and then once we get more comfortable with that and we are able to open up, we will talk about what we are doing in the classroom and is it benefiting children or not. Then that will lead us into discussions of how we teach."

Taking Responsibility for the Operation of the School

As principals involved teachers in decision-making, the teachers increasingly identified decision-making with their own professional duties. At Patricia's school, the teachers fully embraced the annual process of determining the theme for the following school year that would serve as the focus of their work as a faculty. Researchers were happily surprised when on their first visit to Linda's school, they accidentally walked into a meeting of a committee of teachers hashing out the budget for the upcoming school year, without the principal there to lead their discussion. They later received confirmation from the principal that the committee's proposed budget generally went forward just as they had formulated it and became the basis of spending for each school year. The teachers in these schools came to expect to be participants on committees and in study groups, and understood that this work would lead to increased effectiveness of the school.

Valuing Team Work

Teachers could see that creativity and effectiveness were increased when they worked in groups. Although most of them found working in a group or team a little awkward or uncomfortable in the beginning, they came to prefer it once they had learned how to use the team approach effectively. These teachers did not relinquish their individual styles, nor did they decrease personal responsibility. In fact, they were affirmed in their individuality and the contribution they made to the overall creativity of the group. They expressed a willingness to work harder when they saw their colleagues actively pursuing a common goal. These teachers felt free to use their personal styles while their choices for instruction and participation in school operations reflected the identity that the whole school had chosen for itself.

CONCLUDING THOUGHTS

In her work on effective leadership and school change and improvement, Hord (1997b) observes that "as an organizational arrangement, the professional learning community is seen as a powerful staff development approach and a potent strategy for school change and improvement" (p. 1). A principal must be willing to establish a context that nurtures the development of a PLC. Fortunately, some of the principals who have created this context have begun to write about it themselves. When Brian

Riedlinger, an elementary school principal, decided to develop a professional learning community among his staff, he soon realized that he would have to model the practices he wanted from his teachers. "Although I sensed my final objective," Brian writes, "getting to that objective would be my struggle. I suspected that intensive staff development would be the driving force, but my question became, what would I need to do to change *myself* that would lead teachers in the same direction I was moving?" (Riedlinger, 1998, p. 5).

Flo Hill, another successful elementary school principal, writes with two university colleagues:

> No longer are school administrators expected to be merely managers of routines, but must prepare to take initiative. In collaborative school climates, the principal must understand change as well as manage it. Openness to diversity, conflict, reflection and mistakes becomes a necessity. In the facilitative role of fostering collaboration and collegiality, the principal must motivate staff to be dynamically interactive, professionally effective and mission oriented. Thus, knowledge of professional and organizational development and strong interpersonal and communication skills are critical components. (Hill, Lofton, & Chauvin, 1995, pp. 1–2)

To address increasingly complex responsibilities, some principals have created communities of staff learners. These principals use their leadership role to demonstrate and encourage continuous learning for themselves and all staff members. In so doing, they increase the effectiveness of their schools.

CHAPTER 5

The Role of Trust Building and Its Relation to Collective Responsibility

Grace L. Fleming and Tara Leo Thompson

When SEDL researchers examined the confidence and effectiveness of teachers in PLC schools, the strength of the collective responsibility of the staff emerged as a key indicator of that efficacy (Fleming, 1999). In PLC schools, school change or improvement is not dependent on one individual—even the principal—nor is it dependent on a new program or a new curriculum. Instead, school improvement becomes an ongoing focus in which all staff members take collective responsibility. When all staff members take collective responsibility, each teacher's practice is enhanced in a school environment that encourages colleagues to consistently bring and learn new skills and knowledge that will meet their students' needs and ensure student success.

A key question remains to be answered: "How do we create a culture where all staff members take collective responsibility?" In this chapter we examine the role of trust and its relationship to building teacher collective responsibility. It is our contention that when principals build trust with staff and staff build trust with each other, a culture is created where teachers take collective responsibility for ensuring every student's success.

THE IMPORTANCE OF TRUST

How does this culture of collective responsibility develop? All indications point to the principal as the starting point. Schools are able to create professional learning communities because principals are able to move beyond traditional roles to a role that includes actively sharing leadership and encouraging collective learning among teachers (Astuto, Clark, Read, McGree, & Fernandez, 1993; Leithwood, Leonard, & Sharratt, 1997; Sergio-vanni, 1994).

In order for principals to share leadership effectively, there must be a high level of trust among all who are involved. Before teachers and other staff members commit their time and energy to learn new practices, they must trust their administrator and school system to provide the opportunities necessary for them to become confident users of the new knowledge. Once they begin to apply their new knowledge, other staff members must be trusted to support these educators as they take the risks necessary for practicing and mastering their new learning. As Bryk and Schneider (1996) explain,

> (P)roductive collective actions are more likely to occur when relational trust is present among organizational members. . . . (R)elational trust creates an environment where individuals share a moral commitment to act in the interests of the collectivity. . . . This ethical basis for individual action constitutes a moral resource that the institution can draw upon to initiate and sustain change. (pp. 33–34)

In SEDL's research of the development of professional learning communities, the strength of relationships between administrators and staff and among staff members at schools that are operating as PLCs has proven to be critical. The strength of those relationships provides the foundation for all PLC activities. Where PLCs have developed successfully, these relationships include high levels of trust.

This chapter addresses two questions of particular interest to schools that seek to create professional learning communities:

1. How does trust between administrators and staff and among staff motivate staff to engage in learning about more effective ways to teach?
2. How is trust built within a school to encourage teachers to take the risks needed to learn about and implement those improved practices thoroughly?

LESSONS FROM FIVE PRINCIPALS AND THEIR TEACHERS REGARDING TRUST

In the five schools studied, SEDL researchers found principals using shared leadership practices to motivate and authorize staff members to increase their responsibility for the effectiveness of the schools. The teachers' responses indicated trust had been or was being built with the principal.

Furthermore, these principals actively supported teachers by providing resources as the teachers increased or began collective learning and application practices. As the teachers increased their collective responsibility through their learning and application, their trust in each other increased. The result of this greater trust between principal and teachers and among teachers was greater teacher efficacy, as demonstrated by their belief in their power to influence student learning and their willingness to research and initiate school improvement practices.

Research indicates that the process for increasing collective responsibility and therefore increasing teacher efficacy is twofold (Reiss & Hoy, 1998; Smylie & Hart, 1999). Using SEDL's definition of professional learning community, this twofold process can be described as concentrating in the dimensions of shared and supportive leadership and collective learning and application. In the five schools studied, SEDL found that the principals were indeed using these two particular avenues to establish trust within the school.

Supportive leadership is the dimension of a PLC where trust is developed between the principal and teachers within a school. Every principal has a distinctive manner of expressing his or her leadership philosophy. That expression of leadership is demonstrated by the principal's leadership practice. Those principals who succeeded at implementing learning communities were supportive of their teachers and shared leadership as part of their individual leadership practice. It was in this practice of sharing and supporting leadership that principals were earning the trust of their teachers.

These same principals then encouraged trust between and among teachers by engaging them in collective learning and application. The principals established structures for teachers to discover and study effective classroom practices and to apply selected new practices across the school. In this way, two levels of trust were nurtured: that between principal and teachers, and that between and among teachers.

Principals Build Trust with Teachers

As previously indicated, principals initiated the development of trust throughout their schools by first nurturing trust between themselves and their teachers. In professional learning communities, the behaviors and actions that demonstrated this tended to concentrate in the supportive and shared leadership dimension. When the data from the study sites were examined, it was found that many of the actions of the five principals fell into this dimension. Across the five schools, teachers provided numerous examples of their principals inviting teachers to play a role in decision-making about their schools and using their principal roles to support teacher-led initiatives (see Table 5.1).

This notion of sharing leadership authority as part of leadership responsibility sounds perfect, and in an idyllic world it makes sense to include everyone in decision-making. However, the reality of carrying out this practice is quite challenging as the participants learn how to do it.

No one is more heavily impacted than the principal when leadership is shared this way. To their credit, these five principals all had examples of decisions that staff committees and whole-staff meetings had rendered that differed from what the principal believed should be done. Yet the principals knew that deferring to the larger group was indication of trust in the group's capacity for effective decision-making. Interestingly, none of the principals expressed regret for having supported those decisions, and the teachers readily proclaimed having been positively affected by the principal's display of confidence in the staff.

Those shared leadership activities that built trust between administrators and teachers also reflected practices that intersected with three of the other dimensions: shared values and vision, supportive conditions, and collective learning and application.

Shared Values and Vision. The principals maintained a focus on the common vision and values that provided a basis from which all teachers worked. The Cottonwood Creek principal had the school's vision statement read over the public address system daily. The Rolling Hills principal facilitated a deeply collaborative process to develop a mission statement for the school. All five principals were identified as leaders who kept the students' best interests at the center of all decisions at their schools. Violet Canyon teachers knew their principal would compare all major decisions made by teachers to the school's vision statement. At Bayou Bend and Green Valley, the teachers knew their principals would ask how decisions benefited students. Teachers and principal alike referred many times to the litmus test that the staff at Green Valley called their "first filter" when making decisions: "If it's good for kids, it's possible; if it's not good for kids, we don't need to do it."

Supportive Conditions. The schools involved in this study created supportive conditions necessary to maintain their professional learning communities, and the principals were often credited with having provided for or allowed those supportive conditions to exist. Some examples of this included decisions to relocate classes to facilitate interaction between

Table 5.1. Principals Build Trust with Teachers

Activity	Cottonwood Creek	Bayou Bend	Violet Canyon	Green Valley	Rolling Hills
Principal Action	P set up several decision-making teams so teachers could be represented	P took decisions about schooling to Ts to decide programs, activities, schedules, etc.	P established leadership council and design teams so Ts could make decisions about school	P organized campus-based steering committee and worked with entire staff on school-wide improvement initiatives	P built a strong committee structure on which all faculty served to make decisions for the school
Teacher Response	Ts met regularly in these decision-making teams and shared with entire staff	Ts decided on topics for faculty study and brought new ideas to try in classrooms	Ts made major decisions in their design teams about school-wide issues, i.e. had decision-making and budget control over staff development	Ts decided on focus area based on middle school student needs	Ts developed a school-wide curriculum focus, school-wide classroom management process, and implementation of inclusion system
Principal Action	P regularly sat in on grade-level meetings and visited classrooms	P frequently visible in hallways, classrooms, faculty meetings, and consulted with teachers	P had open door policy—available to staff anytime	P visible in hallways and visiting classrooms—willing to substitute so teachers can meet	P began practice of holding whole-school assemblies and meeting with entire faculty every week
Teacher Response	Ts noted that P was available and helpful to them	Ts noted that P knew what was in each teacher's growth plan and knowledgeable about research in education	Ts noted that P was an incredible resource of knowledge—could go to P for help and guidance	Ts noted that P was available to them anytime and knowledgeable about team building	Ts noted that P was available to help them anytime and was a great resource
Principal Action	P repeated vision statement every morning over P.A. system	P continually encouraged staff to maintain focus on what was best for students	P ensured that school vision guided team decisions	P based decisions on educational soundness and benefit to students	P facilitated an extensive collaborative process for the entire staff to develop a mission statement
Teacher Response	Ts operated on belief that their students could be successful	Ts based own learning on students' needs	Ts developed rubric to ensure that instruction and professional development supported vision	Ts adapted to student needs—created family clusters to get to know students	Ts participated in implementation of inclusion system, believing all students can learn

teachers who would work together. The most common form of this strategy was to put teachers of the same grade level near each other in order to facilitate interaction before, after, and through the school day. As noted in Chapter 4, at Violet Canyon, the principal brought the Special Education classes from portable buildings into the main building in order to demonstrate a commitment to fully include those teachers in all facets of school operations and collegiality.

Another strategy principals used to establish supportive structures and systems within the school was to increase communication with and between teachers. Examples of this strategy were weekly all-staff meetings and weekly or monthly newsletters. Some principals established committees of teachers to take responsibility for major areas of school operation such as professional development, technology, and school climate. These committees met regularly or as needed and their charge generally involved decisions about policy, specific actions or events, instructional practices, and finances.

A key factor of supportive conditions was the designation of time on a daily, weekly, or monthly basis, for all or some of the teachers to study and learn together. The time was sometimes designated for a particular topic and other times evolved into study of topics identified by the group's natural evolution from one area of interest to another. In all cases the study related to increased student learning.

Collective Learning and Application. The designation of time for collective learning and application of learning was important both for the principals to build trust with their teachers and to encourage the development of trust between the teachers. This practice was structured differently at each school but with similar effects across the schools. To further emphasize the importance of ongoing professional development or learning, each of these principals modeled an appreciation for learning by constantly reading and making use of opportunities to learn from colleagues and experts. The principals subsequently discussed with teachers their learning and how it might be applied in their school. The teachers talked about their principals as possessing a wealth of knowledge and resources gained by their own ongoing professional development. This observation and appreciation of their principals as continuous learners further strengthened teachers' trust in their principals.

Teachers Build Trust with Each Other

With trust beginning to be established between the principals and the staff through shared leadership, the principals turned to another dimension of

PLC development in order to reinforce the results. While it was important for teachers to participate fully in decision-making and implementation of decisions at the school, it was of equal importance that they be equipped to do that work. One means of avoiding setting them up for failure in their new responsibilities was for the principal to guide them to understand that they could learn from and teach each other by focusing their attention collectively on issues that they identified themselves. This collective learning and application took different forms at the schools (see Table 5.2) but with similar results in all cases. Whether it was a half day once a month, or an hour once a week, the teachers learned to use the time to improve the effectiveness of their instruction. Of significance was that as the teachers engaged in this practice they learned more about each other professionally and personally and in that process their trust in each other grew dramatically.

As teachers, under the guidance of their principals, began to engage in collective learning and application, they continued to operate within three of the other dimensions. Those three dimensions that intersected with collective learning in all five schools were shared leadership, shared values and vision, and supportive conditions. As some staffs grew comfortable in their collective learning format, they eventually took early steps toward engaging in shared personal practice.

Supportive and Shared Leadership. All of the schools in the study continued working on sharing leadership while developing their skills for collective learning and application. This was demonstrated in various ways. In some schools, such as Rolling Hills and Cottonwood Creek, committees of teachers had responsibility for determining how professional development funds were spent—which included official responses to requests by individual teachers for support to attend particular conferences. One factor in those decisions was the importance of the information to be gained in those conferences for the whole staff after the teacher or teachers returned to school. In Cottonwood Creek teachers also worked with the principal to write grants for professional development and other needs of their staff.

In many cases, the purpose of the collective learning and application was for teachers to make decisions or develop materials together, thereby sharing leadership. In Cottonwood Creek teachers worked together to design instructional units for the new curriculum that they had selected. Bayou Bend and Rolling Hills both gave examples of individual teachers discovering new practices that they then brought to the whole staff for examination and possible implementation. Green Valley teachers gathered every spring to determine a dominant theme for

Table 5.2. Teachers Trust Each Other

Activity	Cottonwood Creek	Bayou Bend	Violet Canyon	Green Valley	Rolling Hills
Principal Action	P brought entire faculty together to learn	P brought all of the staff together once a month for faculty study and encouraged staff development for teachers	P believed that staff development and collaboration was essential to a quality school and provided money and time for teachers to access it—early release each week and moved Special Education classes to building for better collaboration	P invested time for staff to get to know one another, guided staff to use early release time for reflection and study, gave staff opportunities to visit other schools and attend conferences, and moved grade-level classes together for better collaboration	P facilitated and promoted a number of whole-faculty learning opportunities and encouraged staff development for teachers
Teacher Response	Ts came together to design new instructional units for new curriculum	Ts sought out their own learning via professional staff development and would bring back learnings to share with school	Ts used early release time to collaborate with other teachers about issues across the school	Ts frequently met in core and cross-grade teams to make decisions and used the early release time to learn from each other	Ts worked together on committees and brought issues back to the staff to look at implementing school-wide
Principal Action	P helped Ts to write grants that supported their work and sent Ts to conferences and professional meetings	P was constantly reading and attending conferences and meetings and sharing that knowledge with staff	P engaged in own learning through reading articles and attending conferences and bringing well-researched resources into the school	P brought well-researched practices for middle school students to school and facilitated meetings to bring staff together	P brought learning from doctorate program to staff and held conviction that the educational process required that everyone learn
Teacher Response	Ts were willing to write grants and go to conferences and professional meetings because of P's support	Ts open to P sharing knowledge and Ts interested in increasing their own knowledge	Ts were encouraged by their P's willingness to learn and share learning with all staff—allowed for Ts to follow suit	Ts appreciated their P's efforts to bring well-researched practices to them—Ts willing to incorporate learnings	Ts acknowledged their P's attitude to learning, which encouraged Ts to be learners of their practice

their work in the succeeding school year based on the needs of their students.

Shared Values and Vision. Increased student learning was at the center of each of these schools' visions. One of the values that they acquired in their sincere efforts to increase student learning was that all staff members would themselves be learners. Teachers in each of the schools talked about their principals modeling the value of learning by sharing resources and knowledge gained from their own learning. These principals "worked elbow to elbow with their teachers to identify and meet the needs of their students." Shared values, shared leadership, and collective learning were all demonstrated at each school where teachers who attended conferences or visited other schools to observe effective practices knew they were responsible for imparting their new knowledge to the entire staff afterward.

Supportive Conditions. Supportive structural conditions were demonstrated by the fact that the schools committed monies to staff development so that all staff could benefit. Fiscal resources were committed for teachers to attend conferences and visit other schools to observe effective practices. In some schools the principals were known for their ability to squeeze money out of the budget for teacher professional development, while other principals gave authority for staff development funds to a committee of teachers.

Supportive conditions were also demonstrated by establishing working committees. For instance, Violet Canyon developed a layered system of committees where several committees were designated for particular purposes related to instruction and school operations. The chairperson of each committee then represented his or her committee on the School Leadership Council where all of the committee work was coordinated. At Rolling Hills, the teachers identified a focus for the school each year and then determined what committees would be needed to meet student needs and maintain that focus. Their committees addressed issues such as technology, the arts, and school climate, and all teachers worked on at least one committee.

In all of the schools studied, the principals had developed structures for all staff to learn together, although these structures varied from school to school. Some schools committed a half day once a month while others had an hour once a week. The teachers developed a commitment to using this time productively to improve their instructional practices and increase student learning.

Shared Personal Practice. Two of the schools had made some progress in learning to share their personal practice. Because a great deal of
trust is required for individuals to participate willingly in giving and
receiving critiques about their classroom instruction practices, this dimension was not widely observed in the five schools. However, several teachers at Rolling Hills made regular reference to a technique that had been
used the year before when they were videotaped while conducting class.
The tapes were later critiqued with the principal and small groups of
teachers. Violet Canyon was beginning to use the Critical Friends model
of teachers giving feedback to each other about their personal practice.
At the other three schools, teachers generally mentioned consulting other
individual teachers about challenges in their classrooms or with particular
students, but they were not at the point of inviting each other into their
classrooms for observation and feedback.

EVIDENCE OF TRUST AND COLLECTIVE RESPONSIBILITY

The principal at each school was key to establishing trust or ensuring
trust within the school. That was not necessarily an easy job. It required
challenging behaviors such as accepting group decisions that differed
from the principal's personal preference. The teachers could describe a
definite and positive impact from their principal's supporting a staff
decision that they knew differed from the principal's personal preference.
This became an important sign that the principal trusted the staff's judgment. This strategy increased both the capacity and the commitment of
staff for taking responsibility for their schools.

As trust was built, staff members were increasingly willing to invest
in collective responsibility. That collective responsibility in turn nurtured
teacher efficacy. When the principal at Cottonwood Creek gave the teachers the power to decide whether to adopt a new curriculum, the teachers
responded by studying the issue and decided to adopt the new curriculum. The teachers then worked together to implement that curriculum.
But implementation of the new curriculum was not the end of their school
improvement efforts. They continued to examine the results of what they
had done.

Trust is not easy to measure, nor is collective responsibility. However,
the SEDL researchers learned about activities and behaviors that could
be considered indicators of trust and of collective responsibility and heard
statements expressing teacher attitudes to the same effect (see Table 5.3).
For instance, in three of the schools, teachers regularly compared the staff
to a family.

Table 5.3. Evidence of Trust and Collective Responsibility

Activity	Cottonwood Creek	Bayou Bend	Violet Canyon	Green Valley	Rolling Hills
Principal Action	P established a group for staff to be candid in their comments and concerns—P listened and respected their concerns	P recognized and praised Ts and encouraged them to follow their instincts	P supported Ts' decisions and actions that were in the best interest of students	P set tone of support and encouragement	P demonstrated respect for staff and supported them in their personal concerns and professional challenges
Teacher Response	Ts voiced concerns and needs; felt supported	Ts viewed themselves as a family of professionals who could take risks and who, together, could make a difference in student learning	Ts described themselves as a family of professionals working together to impact students positively	Ts referred to themselves as a family and expressed the importance of personal and professional relationships with colleagues	Ts consistently described genuine interest in each other's professional success and personal well-being
Principal Action	P gave Ts power to make decision about adopting new curriculum	P let Ts decide what topics would be discussed in faculty study and encouraged them to bring new programs to share with faculty	P created decision-making teams to empower staff to make the decisions—P sometimes not at meeting	P asked the staff to decide on focus for the year based on student needs	P created a committee structure so that staff could make the major decisions about school-wide needs
Teacher Response	Ts adopted new curriculum and chose to work together to implement it	Ts brought ideas/solutions to the staff for school-wide or individual classroom implementation, i.e., topics for faculty study, teaching schedules, new math program	Ts made decisions in their teams—voiced their opinions and were heard	Ts decided on a focus for the year based on students' needs (voiced their concerns and were heard) and engaged in implementing strategies to meet those needs	Ts took the lead in implementing school-wide programs and they showed initiative in solving their own problems

At Bayou Bend and Green Valley, the teachers were clear in expressing their beliefs that their principals had given them permission to make mistakes as they recommended or tried new practices. By giving staff permission to make mistakes, these two principals removed the threat of failure and replaced it with trust that the teachers would end up with high-quality results. The teachers knew they had this trust and chose to engage in various group decision-making and implementation activities. At Bayou Bend, because they knew their ideas would be received positively, teachers regularly brought forward ideas for faculty study and proposed solutions to issues such as teaching schedules and math instruction. Green Valley teachers determined the school's focus each year based on the concerns voiced by their students and selected and implemented the strategies for meeting the students' needs.

> I always told our staff that they are professionals. No one knows the kids at this school better and no one knows better how to teach them than these folks here. I trusted them to be professional.
> —Principal at Green Valley Middle School

The committee structure at Violet Canyon was instrumental in establishing trust between the principal and the teachers. Once the committees began to operate, the principal empowered their decision-making. She did not have to be present at meetings in order for decisions to be made. The teachers knew that, in general, the principal would support the decisions made in those committees. The teachers responded to the principal's trust in them and worked enthusiastically in their committees. The responsibilities of these committees included budget and spending decisions from which the committee members did not shy away. Their work was couched completely in a sense of collective responsibility.

> A lot of it has to do with the freedom we have as teachers. I think the reason that is so important is because it makes us feel responsible for doing what we're doing and it allows us to grow. It's challenging to have that much freedom. It actually makes us work harder.
> —Teacher at Violet Canyon Elementary School

When the principal at Rolling Hills created the committee structure that empowered the teachers to identify the school's focus and working committees each year, the staff responded with full participation on those committees. As a result, the teachers took the lead in implementing schoolwide programs and they showed initiative in solving their own problems.

Their principal proved her faith in their decisions by procuring additional funds to support them. An example of this was the funding she obtained from the district for the Parents as Teachers program when a committee decided to implement an early childhood program on campus. In time, teachers increased their sense of collective responsibility and, even within the committees, all members became more active in implementation of decisions they had made together rather than leaving the implementation to the committee leaders. A good example was their reaction to low test scores on their state's standardized and mandatory geography test for fifth grade. The teachers shared responsibility for the low scores and developed a school-wide curriculum focus on geography that even included geographical items in assemblies.

> Everybody looks at the test results because we don't really consider the fifth grade test to say what the fifth grade teachers did. It says what we all did. So if we're looking at it and we see a weak spot, then for that spot . . . all of us [are] on the line. And together, we start to try to make sure that kids get it.
> —Teacher at Rolling Hills Elementary School

CONCLUSIONS

Professional learning communities rely on trust in order to function effectively. That trust implies that the principals and teachers are all working together to provide the best education possible for their students. In their work together, they accept responsibility collectively for their school, their practice, and their students' education. The process by which trust is built begins with the principal, who invites teachers to share leadership of the school. The teachers begin to trust the principal as they see that the shared leadership is genuine. The principal engages the teachers in collective learning, perhaps even as they are learning how to share leadership. From that collective learning, the teachers increase their capacity for decision-making and implementation of new practices. Simultaneously, they are building trust with one other.

In order for this process to be successful, principal and teachers alike must relinquish traditional views of their roles and define new roles that are better suited to meeting the needs of their students.

The role of the teacher moves from behind the closed doors of an individual classroom out into the halls and offices—into an openness about instruction and learning and active involvement in all facets of school life. This new role can sound intimidating, but when developed carefully over time, teachers find great comfort and empowerment in this role, and are inspired to assume collective responsibility. Their comfort comes from knowing that the other teachers and the administrators care about them both personally and professionally. Teachers in all five schools talked about that support. They described their work setting as a supportive environment. They also understood that each of them was responsible for maintaining that supportive environment. From that commitment to meeting their responsibilities they constantly sought ways to make their schools better.

CHAPTER 6

Creating and Sustaining a Professional Learning Community: Actions and Perceptions of Principal Leadership

Melanie S. Morrissey and D'Ette Cowan

For many years a major focus for school reform has been upon the principal as the acknowledged leader of change in schools. Principals have been referred to as the critical gatekeepers to school improvement because they control structures and environments that determine how receptive teachers are to change. In the five PLC schools SEDL studied, we saw that a principal's actions to develop the five dimensions were crucial to the creation and sustenance of a professional learning community.

Not only were the principal's actions important, but teachers' perceptions of his or her actions also played an important role in the creation of PLCs. These perceptions determine teachers' willingness to support principals' actions. Without such willingness on the part of teachers, it is highly unlikely that schools can develop into professional learning communities.

DEVELOPING COLLECTIVE VALUES AND VISION

The collective values and vision in a school provide a focus and commitment for the school's ongoing improvement work. In the schools studied, the actions of the principals in this regard were particularly effective in helping teachers become student-focused and using the vision to develop and recruit quality staff.

Becoming Student Focused

At each of the schools, the principal emphasized the desire to "do what is best" for students. The principals modeled this intent consistently through their words, actions, and decisions, and communicated to teachers that their work with students was critically important in achieving a vision of academic success for each and every student.

Although the process for the development of each school's vision varied from site to site, the principal at each school, without exception, supported teacher involvement in the development of the vision. Whether the vision was developed through a formal process or simply by frequent attention and example, there were numerous manifestations of its importance. Principals strongly encouraged teachers to use the school's vision for what they want students to know and be able to do as a lens for classroom and school decisions. Principals expressed the collective vision in routine activities, such as the morning announcements, and in conversations with parents, teachers, students, or community members. Hard work was a norm at each of these sites, where staff regularly committed long hours of planning, both independently and collaboratively, for each day of teaching. These principals utilized the vision as a powerful instrument that communicated the importance of and commitment to teaching and learning.

Teachers described their principals' daily work and dedication as "visionary," evidenced by a willingness to try new and innovative practices, and support teachers' work in the classrooms when it strengthened the collective vision. Teachers stated that the shared school-wide vision provided a guiding light for their work, yet offered them sufficient freedom to act within the collective value system. The vision set parameters for school and classroom decisions and helped to focus and direct teachers' collective and individual professional learning experiences. When asked to express their own guiding vision, the teachers without exception cited their focus on student learning, and addressing student needs to that end. Every decision was evaluated by answering the question, "How does this help students?" or "How will this help us to reach our vision?"

The common pursuit of the vision supported the school community by keeping its focus visible every day. At one of the schools, teachers even incorporated their school's vision into student portfolios and rubrics. One teacher stated: "Teachers bend over backwards here to help kids." The staff repeatedly acknowledged a deep commitment to making every day count for their students and themselves.

Using the Vision to Develop and Recruit Quality Staff

The process of vision development increased teacher accountability for achieving the vision. At two of the study sites, the teachers' professional growth plans and portfolios reflected the identified vision and were translated into priorities. These priorities were then purposefully incorporated into teacher evaluation processes and became the core emphasis for the everyday teaching and learning that took place in classrooms.

The principal at Violet Canyon focused on the vision when hiring new teachers and utilized the interview process as an opportunity to identify teachers who wanted to teach in the type of school that she and the staff envisioned. Thus, new staff came into the school more ready and willing to work toward established school priorities.

SUPPORTING SHARED DECISION-MAKING

A second common element among the study sites was that of shared and structured decision-making. These were not schools where the principal made all the decisions alone. Rather, the principals established structures and processes for shared decision-making, promoted shared decision-making on substantive issues, and increased decision-making capacity.

Establishing Structures and Processes for Shared Decision-Making

The principal at each of the schools took the initiative to develop a system for involving teachers in decision-making. Some systems were more highly defined than others, but at each school the teachers could clearly articulate the processes used to make decisions. At Cottonwood Creek, for example, teachers referred to the "ladder of decision-making" to describe who had responsibility for most decisions in the school. At Violet Canyon, "design teams" and grade-level teams provided important feedback to the school leadership council before final decisions were made.

While establishing structures for decision-making was an important step at these schools, of equal importance were the processes the principals initiated to make the structures function effectively. At the beginning, most teachers did not have experience with site-based decision-making, and principals often had to provide training on new roles and responsibilities. The principal at Green Valley taught her staff how to work together as a team, ensure everyone's input, and make group decisions. Other principals requested that teams report what was accomplished at their meetings. This was an important process for keeping staff and administrators informed of team decisions. This type of training paid off with the development of staff cohesiveness in communication and problem solving. Teachers at Violet Canyon stated, "We have a voice in deciding what is best for students and how we can best meet their needs. It's more meaningful," and "The input we have on the decisions that we make has made our school much more productive, not only for staff but for our students."

Promoting Shared Decision-Making on Substantive Issues

Decisions given over to the staff at all the school sites were substantive ones, on topics such as budget allocation, staff development, scheduling, curriculum adoption, student assessment, and student incentives. At each of the schools, all major decisions were brought to the whole staff before action was taken. The principal at Cottonwood Creek stated that her goal was to "empower the faculty and cause them to take greater responsibility for decisions made and the direction the school will take." Although she oversaw the school improvement plan, teachers participated fully in its development. This principal, as well as the others, stressed the need to use data for making informed decisions and helped their staff learn how to find and use data to examine issues and evaluate the outcomes of decisions. Such processes helped assure that decisions would be made with appropriate data and according to their school's vision.

Teachers responded to the call of decision-making by contributing thoughtfully and purposefully to decisions made for their campuses, while also acknowledging the authority role of the principal as leader. They used the school's vision as a filter for all decision-making, and worked together to examine data to help lead them toward a common goal. One Green Valley teacher, for example, described how the staff at her school deliberated on the best use of limited resources: "We divided up the budget without bickering, and gave allocation to the departments as needed."

Regardless of the structures and processes for including teachers in decision-making at their schools, teachers felt their input on substantive issues was valued and that their principals trusted the teachers to make good decisions. All players stayed true to the decision-making process, and there was no "pulling rank." Teachers, in turn, trusted their principals to support and honor their decisions.

Increasing Decision-Making Capacity

Of equal importance to establishing shared decision-making structures was the ability of the principals to increase decision-making capacity among their staff. In cases where decision-making experience was initially absent, the principals identified key teachers with whom they worked to develop their experience.

Teachers reacted favorably to opportunities for shared decision-making, particularly on issues that impacted their everyday work. Teachers repeatedly cited their role in the decision-making process, and referred to their increased sense of empowerment by being involved in school decision-making. For instance, teachers at Bayou Bend helped the principal develop a schedule that eliminated departmentalization on campus. Teachers here were accustomed to a former principal who was "unilateral" in decision-making and admitted that when the current principal tried to shift some of the decision-making responsibility to the staff, they initially "felt pushed to do things they didn't want to do." However, once those teachers became involved in the new processes, they were more than willing to roll up their sleeves and get busy in the process of improving their school. A teacher at Green Valley noted that shared decision-making has resulted in a feeling among her colleagues that they no longer work *for* someone, but rather *with everyone*.

Teachers grew professionally as a result of the site-based decision-making opportunities afforded them. They began to identify the emergence of teacher leadership among their ranks and admitted to "taking over control of things and developing ownership" for the decisions that affected their school. They also began to take initiative in decision-making that reflected their dedication to their vision, their students, and their school. The results were a stronger sense of involvement in, responsibility for, and freedom in the decisions made to support the work of the school.

PROMOTING CONTINUOUS LEARNING

Another important characteristic of all five schools studied, for both students and staff, was the emphasis on continuous learning. The actions of principals in this category were particularly effective in communicating the value of learning, encouraging ongoing self-analysis, and connecting professional development to school-improvement goals.

Communicating the Value of Learning

Setting the tone for the whole school, the principals not only encouraged teachers to be continuous learners, but were also learners themselves. Professional development for staff came through formal and informal opportunities, from days set aside specifically for the entire staff to learn something new, to after-school hours dedicated to learning new strategies for teaching reading. The principals supported such professional development and also provided the opportunities and resources to do so. For example, the principal at Violet Canyon strongly supported the allocation of all monies possible from various title programs and other sources to staff development. Other principals arranged for teachers to visit each other's classrooms or different schools to learn new strategies in teaching and assessment. The principals themselves also regularly engaged in their own professional development, reading research, attending conferences and meetings, and bringing the learning back to share with their staffs.

Teachers utilized the opportunities for learning by dedicating regular planning times to work with grade-level team members, discussing classroom teaching strategies, sharing ideas, planning together, and problem-solving. Over time, the formal and informal processes for staff to learn together, were perceived as necessary for continuous improvement. One teacher commented, "It has really challenged us as educators to grow and to keep working to better ourselves." Teacher interdependence was developed and valued as teachers learned, shared, and worked together. Principals encouraged staff to participate in professional development activities and then share their learning with the entire faculty. Several principals also regularly encouraged staff to share existing or new practices in their classrooms, acknowledging that teachers too infrequently have opportunity to learn from their colleagues' daily practice.

Teachers also held high expectations of each other for learning. At each of the schools in the study, teachers committed to meeting regularly with grade-level teams as a means of learning with and from colleagues. While this often meant meeting after school hours, teachers allocated the time because they valued the expertise and interaction that came from working in a group. Although teachers were not required to attend these meetings, they so valued learning that there was a tacit expectation for everyone's involvement.

Monitoring Growth and Progress

Much of the value placed on learning at these school sites was reflected in the willingness of the staff to continually assess where they were in relation to their goals. Principals supported activities that required teachers to analyze their classroom practice. From working together to implement a new curriculum and align it with state test standards, to bringing in different models for examination, the principals subtly asked teachers to continually reflect on their practice and identify areas for improvement. At the same time, administrators were supportive of teachers taking risks in an effort to accomplish their professional goals. Principals supplied the necessary data or information for teachers to use for self-analysis, and to guide the staff through reflection activities for this purpose.

Teachers responded positively to administrative requests for learning through self-analysis of classroom or school-wide practice. In most cases, the staff felt that such assessment was a natural extension of the classroom, where they monitor and assess student progress on a daily basis. Teachers recalled times when they were dissatisfied with the progress students were making, or with a particular curriculum in use, and used that dissatisfaction as an opportunity to investigate new ideas or strategies that might serve them better. For example, at Green Valley, teachers took their state assessment data, identified students scoring below a satisfactory mark, and targeted them for extra assistance in the problem areas. Constantly assessing and monitoring their work, as well as that of students, helped them to continuously get better and better at doing what was best for kids.

Connecting Professional Development to School Improvement Goals

In every case, the schools' collective vision guided the professional development of the staff. Principals required decision-making teams to use the vision as a guide for determining appropriate staff development and improvement activities. Two school administrators utilized opportunities with externally offered programs that met the goals of the school improvement plan to increase student gains and develop staff as a collaborative unit. One school implemented student advisory and interdisciplinary teaming because they found data to support that decision. In every case, the administrator assisted staff through problem-solving and long-term planning when identifying the relationship of professional development to school-improvement goals.

Teachers valued the alignment of the school's improvement efforts with their professional development goals. Faculty studies and professional development that related to the needs of the teachers and the school-improvement plans were initiated. Staff were not looking for a "magic pill" to solve their problems. Instead, teachers found solutions by learning and working together toward a common goal, realizing that such learning and change take time and effort.

Continuous learning at these schools was not motivated by crisis or mandate. Rather, it was embedded in the culture established, supported by principals, and incorporated by teachers, so that schoolwide expectations were promoted for everyone on staff. Learning was valued at every stage, at every level, and was ongoing throughout the teaching process. Teacher interdependence was supported, and contributed to making stronger, better functioning staff across the sites.

ENCOURAGING COLLABORATION

As professional development is highly valued in professional learning communities, so is the continuous learning that is nurtured through collaboration among teachers. Principals in these professional learning communities provided time and support for collaboration, and identified outcomes for staff collaboration.

Providing Time and Support for Collaboration

As mentioned previously, the principal is key in finding and allocating time for teachers to collaborate on student learning issues. Some of the sites or school districts had collaborative time for teachers built into their regular schedules. In most cases, however, these administrators had to be very flexible and creative in providing collaboration time. Early release days on the district calendar initially offered collaboration time for Green Valley, but when the practice was discontinued, the principal found other ways to provide time for teachers to work together. She used evening meetings to share information with the staff, often providing dinner, or asking the teachers to potluck. This ensured the regularly scheduled during- and after-school time would be free for collaboration, rather than taken up by administrative issues. Another principal provided substitutes for teachers to go off-campus during the school day to plan various things. Bayou Bend's administrator volunteered to substitute for her teachers in the classroom during the day, in order to provide the necessary time for collaboration.

Although initial use of the collaborative time required substantial guidance from principals, over time and with the maintenance of a clear vision, teachers knew where they were going and what they needed to do with that time. Teachers readily acknowledged spending a good deal of time meeting together, but all felt it was beneficial for themselves and their students. A teacher from Rolling Hills stated: "When we work the best and function the best and are the most successful is when we have time to plan together." When asked to meet together after school hours, almost all teachers participated because they valued the time provided to work together. In several cases, teachers participated "above and beyond the call of duty" to make time for collaboration. For example, a group of 34 teachers from Green Valley volunteered to spend 2 hours every Thursday to attend a reading class over a period of 20 weeks. The teachers involved in this extended workshop agreed that the most beneficial part of the experience was that they were learning together and had time to collaborate and plan for the implementation of their learning.

Identifying Outcomes of Collaboration

The principals placed value on providing collaborative time for teachers and clearly communicated their expectations for rigorous use of that time. Principals sometimes called meetings specifically to establish the expectations for collaborative time and shared processing and brainstorming strategies that could facilitate the collaborative process. In the beginning, some principals guided the planning time by offering teachers information and/or resources on new programs, ideas, or test scores. Principals frequently checked in with grade-level or other collaborative groups in order to determine whether there were any needs or questions that they could assist with. Not only did this strategy let the administrator know what was going on during that collaborative time, but it also supported the work of the teachers.

The teachers used the processes learned in their large-group discussions and applied them to their smaller, collaborative settings. These tools helped them to be more efficient and effective, and make the most of this "captured" time. Teachers spoke of "monitoring and adjusting" their instructional practices according to feedback from their peers during these times and felt that their work in the collaborative settings positively influenced and benefited the students. One teacher summed up the perceived value of collaborative work by stating: "We enhance learning by working together instead of working separately."

Initial guidance from the principal was necessary for the staff to learn how to most effectively and productively use time together. However, staff initiative was taken to apply that learning to other collaborative situations productively over time.

PROVIDING SUPPORT

The final, and likely most critical, characteristic identified in this study is that of support. The aspect of support is the most subtle characteristic found at the five study schools, although the role it plays in strengthening the growth and development of professional learning communities cannot be ignored. Principals provided support in numerous ways: assisting teachers by establishing clear expectations, developing relationships, devising systems for communication, and acknowledging the human capacity for change.

Establishing Clear Expectations

The principals of these sites provided ongoing support by assisting the staff in developing a common vision, and then acting as initial "keeper" of the vision. Using their vision as the backbone for the work done in the schools, principals encouraged and nurtured whole-school collaboration on major decisions, and consistently worked to build an environment of trust and risk-taking. Administrators established clear expectations by acting as advocates for children and facilitators of adult learning. One teacher summed up the level of expectations held on his campus by stating: "The principal believes that teachers working collaboratively can improve themselves and the instruction we deliver, and she wants an environment where that can and will happen."

Teachers were appreciative of their principals' expectations—they felt supported, but not as though the principal was always "leading the charge." They were comfortable working within the normal parameters of leadership, with regard to decisions and responsibilities, and regularly checked with the principal to confirm alignment of their actions with the school's vision. At each school site, there were also similarly high expectations held between the teachers themselves. Not only were teachers willing to commit the necessary time and energy to pursue their best work on behalf of students, but they also continually provided mutual support for each other in their own teaching and learning. When there were issues, problems, or concerns, teachers rallied together to find the best solution. They saw themselves as "members of a team working together as a family of professionals."

Developing Relationships

Not only did the principals make connections with staff, recognizing and praising their work both publicly and privately, but they also often created opportunities for staff to get to know each other outside of the school setting. In an attempt to acknowledge the "wholeness" of each teacher, to get to know one another on a personal basis, principals provided monthly breakfasts, retreats, and other social-type events. Administrators consciously attended to the personal dimensions of teachers' lives, celebrating birthdays, births, and other personal events, and including families in annual events. Principals were also very visible throughout the school. They each had an "open-door policy" and were regularly available to teachers, students, and parents alike.

Teachers responded to the opportunities provided by learning about one another and developing trust and respect. The words "family" and "community" came up often in interviews as teachers described their schools' atmosphere. Staff were comfortable having disagreements, as families often do, and utilized those opportunities as times to grow and learn from each other. The differences among staff, whether it was in experience, expertise, or heritage, was honored, enjoyed, and celebrated.

Devising Structures for Communication

An easily neglected factor in many schools, the systems for communication at the study sites were timely, efficient, and succinct. Morning announcements took care of daily issues for staff and students; and daily bulletins, e-mails, or memos communicated to teachers issues specifically pertinent to their practice. There were also school newsletters, often developed by the principal, or by individual classrooms, that kept parents informed of the work in the schools.

Teachers often used bulletin boards to communicate meeting minutes, and e-mail was used frequently by teachers to discuss daily work, collaboration times, future events, and general announcements.

Acknowledging the Human Capacity for Change

Familiar with the demands of the change process, the principals constantly monitored how much their teachers could take on at one time. They found ways to provide the necessary balance between pressure and support in order for their teachers to experience success. Administrators at these schools developed structures and processes for dealing with the stress and conflict of change and learning. At Cottonwood Creek, the principal set up monthly meetings called "Charettes" to provide teachers with a place where they could vent their concerns and be heard. At Bayou Bend, each new teacher was assigned a mentor, with the intent of helping new staff to assimilate to the somewhat demanding atmosphere of the professional learning community. Violet Canyon's principal encouraged and supported informal teams to work together in problem solving and support each other. At each site, there was a strategy for giving teachers enough space to learn at their own pace.

Teachers at the schools valued the experiences and expertise that each other provided when working toward a common goal. One teacher confirmed the level of comfort and trust at her school by stating the following: "We are allowed to say, okay change is hard, but change isn't bad. We could voice our opinions if we were uncomfortable." Teachers felt encouraged to step out of their comfort zones and try new things, understanding that they were supported in risk-taking. A teacher from

Bayou Bend summed up the support she and her colleagues felt by saying, "To get a school like this you have to have . . . a principal who is willing to let people take it at whatever baby steps they need to take it in."

Within these professional learning communities, support was provided to everyone, relationships were developed and nurtured, and diversity was accepted, encouraged, and celebrated. The principals' clear expectations led to confidence in decision-making and follow-through on responsibilities, and teachers were allowed to learn and work at a comfortable pace.

WHAT DOES THIS MEAN FOR SCHOOL IMPROVEMENT?

The results of this study reflect a significant change in perspective regarding the roles of teachers and administrators, and provide examples of how professional learning communities can be developed to support school improvement. While these finding have been presented in a positive light, focusing on the supportive and nurturing actions of principals and teachers, it is also important to acknowledge that the transformations these schools experienced were not without the conflict and dissension that are a natural part of the change process. What set them apart was the ability of each staff to learn how to deal with the normal reactions to change together, and to collectively use that learning to respond in an effective manner, while continuing to move forward in their growth as a professional learning community.

Professional learning communities exist when an administrator's actions are positively perceived and reciprocated by the teachers on staff. The principal's role is a critical one, orchestrating a delicate interaction between support and pressure, encouraging teachers to take on new roles while themselves letting go of old paradigms regarding the role of school administrator. In the case of this study, the creation of professional learning communities at these schools required significant endorsement from the principals by developing shared values and vision, supporting shared decision-making, promoting continuous learning, encouraging collaboration, and providing support. The weight of responsibility for improvement and renewal is shared equally with the faculty, and engages the voices of all professional staff.

School staff within professional learning communities are continually engaged in reflection, inquiry, problem solving, and learning and teaching together. A common vision guides every aspect of the work they do, and every substantive decision that is made. Regular opportunities are not only provided, but also sought, to learn and grow in the profession, enriching the regular collaboration among teachers necessary for continual growth. Teachers who are part of this kind of community prize the sharing of knowledge, expertise, and experiences, creating an environment that values hard work, risk-taking, and personal growth.

Substantive change is never simple, and any change requires learning. Progress can only be made when the administrators and teachers on a school staff find ways to go beyond the historical perceptions and traditional structures within education to significantly impact the teaching-learning process. Principals and teachers both play major roles in this endeavor; changes of this magnitude require an emphasis on continuous learning and inquiry, and transforming a school to engage teachers in such work demands a great deal of support from principals.

CHAPTER 7

Creating Co-Developers: Linking Research and Practice

D'Ette Cowan and Anita Pankake

As seen in previous chapters, SEDL staff learned about the value and characteristics of professional learning communities through the first phase of the Creating Communities of Continuous Inquiry and Improvement project. But we still did not fully understand how PLCs were established in schools. To promote PLCs not just as a "grand idea," but as a way to organize schools for increased student achievement, we first needed to find out more about the knowledge, skills, and practices necessary to create PLCs.

SEDL's review of the professional literature and its many years of experience working with practitioners in the field helped to inspire the idea for the second phase of the CCCII project. Why not invite participants from the Leadership for Change Cadre, a previous SEDL project, to participate in fleshing out the design and implementation of a project that would increase understanding about creating PLCs while doing this work in schools? Thus was born the second phase of the CCCII project—the idea of creating a corps of education professionals, called *co-developers*, who were able and willing to enter schools as external agents of change.

This chapter describes (1) how potential co-developers were identified, (2) how they were prepared for their work, and (3) by illustrative references, how SEDL, the newly trained co-developers, and participating schools began the pilot test of the grand idea—public schools as real-world examples of professional learning communities.

IDENTIFYING THE CO-DEVELOPERS AND THEIR ROLES

In the fall of 1997, SEDL invited selected colleagues known to have special interest in school improvement to join the CCCII project. Thirty individuals—from higher education faculties, state departments of education, intermediate education agencies, local education agencies, campuses, and other regional education laboratories—expressed an interest in participating in the project. Although attracted to the project for different reasons, they each held an abiding interest in increasing student learning within an environment that supports and nurtures the learning of the professionals who are responsible for that student learning.

Even with the initial invitation, these potential co-developers in the CCCII project were asked to think about field sites for the implementation of creating a PLC. In some cases, co-developers were already familiar with a school due to a history of interaction in another capacity (e.g., as an intermediate technical assistance provider from a service center or as a consultant). In two cases, co-developers were principals of schools selected for the project. Additionally, the co-developers were asked to make a commitment of 3 years to the project. Even so, as mentioned in Chapter 1, attrition to the co-developer ranks occurred over the 3 years. At the end of the project, 19 co-developers remained, and not all of them were still working in their selected field sites.

The work that SEDL proposed for co-developers was not for the faint of heart. They would be asked to embark on a journey of discovery to understand better how to create PLCs at a time when very little information existed about how to do such work. And, in doing so, they would be expected to act in four roles:

1. *As colleagues in a professional learning community of co-developers.* SEDL recognized the importance of giving co-developer individuals firsthand, experiential learning about what it is like to be part of a PLC, so they might have a meaningful and personal understanding of what PLC is and how it operates.
2. *As external facilitators and field-based developers in schools.* This was the primary role to be played by co-developers to help their schools operate as PLCs. Serving as an external change agent or facilitator is a very demanding role, requiring a wide array of capacities. Their preparation for this role was an imperative.
3. *As contributors to applied research.* The co-developers' ability to maintain records of their plans and the actions taken in the schools and to reflect on the effects of those actions would provide the project with information about what worked and what didn't in creating PLCs. This information would provide the project with both formative and summative assessments.
4. *As disseminators of information about the project to other audiences.* In order to "scale up" the creation of PLCs and the sharing of procedural knowledge for doing so, co-developers would make presen-

tations at conferences and publish in education journals so that this information would be widely available.

Once the invitations were extended and accepted, the major first step in the second phase of the CCCII project was completed. Next on the agenda was to help the selected co-developers learn the necessary skills for fulfilling the four roles that each would be expected to play as the implementation of the project continued. Identifying what needed to be learned, by whom, and how best to assure the necessary learning were issues that consumed the SEDL staff and the co-developers themselves for the next several months.

PREPARING CO-DEVELOPERS FOR THEIR WORK

Although knowledgeable in their own areas of expertise and experience, none of the participants entered the study with *all* the skills they would require as co-developers. SEDL immediately began a series of meetings and activities to develop these skills among the co-developers, and to teach the co-developers about professional learning communities through assisting them in forming a PLC among themselves. The following sections describe the preparation of co-developers in each of the roles.

As Colleagues in the Professional Learning Community of Co-Developers

Co-developers first came to SEDL's Austin headquarters in November 1997 for an overview of the 3-year project and an introduction to the concept of the PLC. SEDL provided descriptive research (both their own and that of others) that illustrated the power of school staffs as communities of learners. SEDL also engaged co-developers in dialogue that led them to share and develop their visions of school improvement through PLC structures and relationships, and to recognize the potential for increased student learning through such structures and relationships.

In addition, SEDL supported co-developers in creating a professional learning community among themselves, by supporting co-developer activities and abilities along each of the five PLC dimensions: supportive and shared leadership, shared values and vision, collective learning and application of that learning, supportive conditions, and shared personal practice.

Supportive and Shared Leadership. Allowing co-developers to choose their schools, regardless of the school's readiness for change, provided them with an early and significant experience of personal authority and consequence. Each co-developer was to make an overture to his or her selected school site; yet how that was done varied with the uniqueness of the site administrators and the individual co-developer. As co-developers set their individual courses, they took on the responsibility for finding their own way. These variations for selecting school sites provided important learning for co-developers and helped generate data for the larger project mission in understanding how gaining site entry might best be accomplished.

SEDL did not abandon co-developers, however, in preparing them for the work ahead with the selected sites. The SEDL staff provided support through communication, resources, and research materials, and by connecting co-developers and building their school improvement facilitation skills. This process built capacity and confidence by acknowledging the varied existing skills of the co-developers. The process of identifying and sharing such knowledge and skills for serving as successful change agents was an integral part of nurturing leadership among co-developers. Permitting co-developers to define their own roles in the planning and presentation of later conferences allowed for further leadership development.

Shared Values and Vision. A strong commitment to school improvement was evidenced in each of the co-developers, as they volunteered for and continued in the CCCII project. Through dialogue, formal exercises, and informal discussion, SEDL nurtured the co-developer group in coming to greater understanding of the values they shared—namely, democratic structures, courage to make and face change, and commitment to student achievement.

Collective Learning and Application of That Learning. Collective learning and its application were intrinsic to the project design. Sharing needed knowledge and skills informally was a constant between and among co-developers; additionally, some knowledge and skill areas were given specific attention through formal instruction. Co-developers served as leaders in the learning for many of these.

As the project progressed, data from existing research and from site application efforts were gathered and quickly disseminated among co-developers. Time was set aside in every meeting for informal conversation, which often included the sharing of stories, strategies, and advice. In addition, outside research was shared and discussed. SEDL facilitators assisted in the application of strategies from a wide range of sources to the opportunities and problems that arose in the course of this project.

Supportive Conditions. As much as possible, SEDL took on the task of providing supportive conditions—both structural and human—for the co-developer PLC. Meetings were held in locations convenient for as many co-developers as possible. A listserv was created to make it possible for co-developers to network among themselves. SEDL facilitators provided to co-developers a wide variety of SEDL resources as well as those of other educational institutions by distributing copies of research studies or by referring co-developers to additional resource people.

Shared Personal Practice. As co-developers periodically shared their stories of success, failures, and perplexity in their individual school sites, they solicited feedback from other co-developers. The sharing of experiences at the various sites helped to increase awareness and understanding of potentially successful strategies. Furthermore, co-developers acted as "critical friends" to their colleagues, offering advice and feedback on their approach and interventions at their sites.

While co-developers were unable to visit one another's schools, SEDL facilitators made one visit to each site. Their firsthand observations provided opportunities for co-developers to gain new insights into personal and professional dynamics at their schools, as well as their own role in facilitating change.

As External Facilitators and Field-Based Developers in Their Schools

As external facilitators and change agents, the co-developers' primary job was to foster development of the five PLC dimensions at each school. Because the co-developers' work was so context dependent, it is difficult to generalize how they worked with individual schools. Over the course of the project, contextual factors, particularly those associated with the states and districts in which the schools were located, significantly impacted the co-developers' actions and actions of others associated with the schools. For example, at one district, a federal investigation into the county's handling of grant money and an impending takeover of the district by the state created an atmosphere of suspicion and distrust that filtered into the school. Transitions of principals and superintendents represented another recurring contextual factor that affected the co-developers' work. Of the 19 schools remaining at the end of the project, five had experienced changes of principals during the 2-year period and four others had experienced superintendent changes. Co-developers found it necessary to deal directly with contextual issues such as these to ascertain actions they should take and consequences that were likely to result from their actions.

Much of the co-developers' initial work centered around becoming acquainted with school staff and assessing how the school operated. As change agents, the co-developers often took a "balcony view" (Garmston & Wellman, 1999), a macrocentric view in which they tried with compassion and detachment to understand the situations and contexts that faced the school staffs and encouraged the actions of individuals in new roles to help their school become a PLC. They helped clarify how a staff's action could support the values to which they were committed and challenged administrators to raise expectations, identify resources that could help achieve their goals, and reduce distractions that might take them off course.

Meetings with co-developers throughout the first 6 months of the project were designed primarily to prepare them for work in the field. Very early in the project, in January 1998, SEDL asked co-developers to join with them in identifying the knowledge, skills, and understandings that would prepare them as external facilitators to help schools develop as PLCs. Because creating a PLC in a school was new territory for everyone involved, the specific knowledge, skills and understandings were "best bets" based on existing research and the co-developers' experiences in other school improvement efforts.

Sharing Knowledge and Skills. Meetings in March and in May 1998 provided opportunities for co-developers to share knowledge and skills in such areas as data collection and analysis, dialogue, team building, overcoming resistance, and developing a vision. Co-developers also reflected upon various ways to apply their new learning and expertise, and to make a concrete plan for how they would use each proficiency.

After initial meetings devoted to understanding the PLC dimensions and training in essential skills and knowledge, SEDL encouraged co-developers to finalize the selection of a school with which they wanted to work to develop a PLC. As mentioned previously, in SEDL's view, allowing co-developers to select their own schools would provide a variety of settings for understanding how to create PLCs. Not all of the co-developers were successful in securing the cooperation of a school site. For example, one site was shared by two of the co-developers, and already the attrition of co-developers had begun due to circumstances that included changes in employment and unanticipated job and family demands. Things were changing within the cohort of co-developers even as the change plans in their schools were getting underway.

The following fall, co-developers invited the principal and a lead teacher from each of the 22 participating schools to accompany them to a SEDL conference in Austin. Co-developers collaborated in planning this conference and took an active role in leading various parts of the meeting. With SEDL's support, co-developers introduced the concept of PLCs to a lead teacher and principal from each campus and engaged these professionals in identifying their roles and responsibilities for introducing—and practicing—PLC principles in their schools. The conference was also an opportunity for many of the co-developers to get better acquainted with their principals and lead teachers. It provided them time to plan how they would initiate the project at their school.

At the close of this fall 1998 meeting, SEDL provided each participant with resource materials comprised of tools and strategies for creating PLCs.

SEDL's Supporting Role. At all meetings, SEDL staff modeled principles of professional development that research supports for adult learners. SEDL also provided opportunities for co-developers to reflect on various uses of specific knowledge and skills for different purposes. To support co-developers in their work at schools, SEDL staff were assigned to co-developers to offer assistance on various issues that arose at schools. Each SEDL staff member worked with five to six co-developers and supported co-developers by listening to their frustrations, acting as sounding boards for their ideas about the work in their schools, and suggesting new and innovative ideas. Frequent e-mail and telephone contacts made it possible for SEDL staff to respond quickly to questions and concerns of co-developers. SEDL staff also provided research-based information to help address co-developers' issues as they worked with their schools.

As Contributors to Applied Research

Co-developers provided valuable data toward the project's goal of discovering how PLCs are created. By sharing their stories in oral and written forms, and completing and administering a variety of research instruments, co-developers provided both qualitative and quantitative data. At SEDL conferences, a number of methods—including narratives and photographs developed by co-developers, audiotape recordings of co-developer reports, and observations by SEDL staff—were utilized to capture data from co-developers, principals, and teachers.

The Research Team. Within the larger group of co-developers emerged a smaller group of five co-developers and one SEDL staff member that would come to form the "research team." This team, comprised primarily of individuals in higher education who were interested in writing for publication, first met and began working with one another during the meetings at SEDL. The CCCII project provided these individuals the opportunity to work together as productive and supportive colleagues before and after the larger project came to an end.

The research team played a vital role in the analysis of the information collected through PLC instruments, lending their expertise and time to the triangulation and disaggregation of data. In research team meetings, members shared both data and perspectives leading to new avenues of consideration, new methods of analysis, and new perspectives on the PLC model of school change and improvement. The team then reported their findings to the larger group of co-developers to share with them emergent theories and insights that could assist all in their work with schools. As all research team members provided support to the others in their writing and publishing endeavors, the SEDL facilitator working with the research team also helped to maintain and enhance the connection between these efforts and the larger SEDL project.

Within the smaller research team, as in the larger group of co-developers, emerging friendships developed into powerful professional partnerships. Much of the research team's understanding and practice of PLC interactions were derived from the work in the larger group of co-developers; this knowledge and these skills were then utilized when the research team began its work.

Several research team members collaborated on papers and presentations for conferences and workshops, thus formally comparing their experiences and drawing lessons from one another. Data interpretation activities provided each team member—and the team as a whole—new insights into the realities of developing learning communities. Seeing the complexity of school change through multiple eyes produced deeper understanding and greater appreciation for the difficulties of making change; provided evidence of the promise PLCs can hold in very diverse settings; and persuaded team members that change is possible and that their work can help influence others.

Shared and supportive leadership remained a hallmark of the research team. Members' roles were defined by expertise, not position. The research team valued and utilized the skills of all members, including those who were not involved in higher education. The SEDL project provided a "level playing field" on which these individuals met and cooperated as colleagues.

Among the research team, cooperation, collaboration, and support for others' success quickly emerged as a value shared and sometimes in short supply in their regular work places. These shared values were demonstrated in the commitment that research team members displayed as part of the team—completing tasks on time; attending meetings before, after, and in addition to SEDL meetings; and providing honest and timely feedback on one another's work.

The research team participated in collaborative research, analysis, and writing. They shared stories from their schools in enough detail to assure that all members of the research team were intimately familiar with the progress of one another's schools and the special challenges each of the research team members faced. The trust that developed between members of the research team also allowed conversations to range across the spectrum of members' personal and professional lives, enabling mutual support and sustenance.

A commitment to "do what it takes" to support one another was evident among research team members. One member made her home available for meetings, hosting the entire team for 3 days at a time on multiple occasions. Individually, research team members worked ahead of schedule or declined other projects in order to maintain their commitment and best utilize their time with the research team. Members shared books and articles, edited one another's papers, distributed information about professional organizations, encouraged one another in attending professional conferences, and created opportunities to write and publish collaboratively.

While the focus of the research team was the PLC project, conversations and interactions at their meetings covered myriad personal and professional issues. Members were confident they could share with the group confidential work information and highly personal situations—that they could trust each other with their lives, so to speak.

Tools for Data Collection. SEDL provided co-developers with archival data collection forms and other tools to guide them in documenting important events in the development of their schools as PLCs. As an aid to recording their continuing process, SEDL also developed and provided co-developers with a casebook in which to describe their actions at their schools and results of these actions. The casebook was designed to help co-developers report how their interventions and activities promoted one or more of the five dimensions of a PLC. Co-developers were also encouraged to include descriptions of critical incidents—planned or unplanned, successful or unsuccessful—that they recognized as particularly significant in creating a PLC.

SEDL trained co-developers in the administration of other instruments, including the PLC assessment *School Professional Staff as a Learning Community* (Hord, 1996). SEDL requested that all co-developers first administer the PLC assessment instrument in the fall of 1998 to provide baseline data about how the school staff perceived itself along a continuum of each of the five dimensions of a PLC. Subsequent administrations of the PLC Survey in the fall of 1999 and spring of 1999 measured each school's progress. Co-developers shared the data with their schools, helping the staffs to monitor their own growth and development as professional learning communities.

SEDL also trained co-developers to use an interview protocol to collect perceptual data from school personnel on their progress in becoming professional learning communities. Each interview was audiotaped and transcribed, then analyzed by the research team using the five dimensions of PLCs as a framework for examination. The resulting data provided information that profiled the campus at the initial stage of the project and further helped the co-developers learn about the school.

A Writing Conference. In January 1999, after most of the co-developers had been in their schools for approximately 5 months, SEDL hosted a writing conference in a retreat setting to begin to transform their documentation of interventions and activities into "case stories." As a first step in supporting co-developers' writing, SEDL organized co-developers into five- to six-member teams for verbally exchanging stories with colleagues. In these teams, SEDL coached co-developers in using a structured dialogue protocol for offering encouragement, advice, and feedback to their peers in how to structure their stories in writing. This interaction helped co-developers reflect on their school stories and revise earlier written drafts to include more clarity and detail.

As Disseminators of Information about the Project

SEDL acknowledged each co-developer's professional areas of interest and affiliation and allotted meeting time for co-developer collaboration on ways to disseminate information about the project within the professional organizations to which co-developers belonged.

Formal Dissemination Efforts. Meeting time allocated for this purpose had positive results. Co-developers who represented higher education were particularly interested in pursuing opportunities to disseminate learnings from the project. For example, one co-developer asked SEDL staff to write an article for her state's professional development publication. Another co-developer, the editor of a National School Development Council publication, included articles from SEDL staff and colleague co-developers for an entire issue devoted to PLCs. Other co-developers collaboratively developed and delivered presentations about PLCs and the CCCII project at national conferences such as the American Educational Research Association and the National Staff Development Council conference.

Informal Dissemination Activities. Informal conversation among education professionals has long been recognized as an important influence upon the norms and practices at a school. It would be difficult to measure the informal dissemination of the project that has occurred through conversation and example within schools; yet there is little doubt that conversations of principals and lead teachers in the CCCII project schools have impacted practice and interactions in ways that will outlive this project. Such informal conversations among principals or among district personnel involved in the project with their co-workers represent effective, valuable, and actual methods whereby this project is being explained and explored in educational circles and at other places.

Continuing Dissemination Efforts. The research team provided perhaps the most obvious example of co-developers serving as information disseminators. They continue to work together on their own time and at their own expense, and they remain highly motivated and energized by their ongoing inquiry into PLCs. In 2000, the American Educational Research Association accepted six proposals from the research team. The intensity of effort required to write and deliver these presentations further strengthened the commitment of the researchers to this project and to further understanding of how PLCs can support school improvement.

LESSONS LEARNED FROM "THE GRAND IDEA"

The CCCII project represents an initial effort, and as such has provided some important insights for future research and efforts to create PLCs in schools. New SEDL projects have incorporated many of the lessons learned from this early exploration.

The Concept of Co-Developers

The concept of co-developer was found to have some real merit as a mechanism for linking research and practice. Individuals from various positions and backgrounds successfully fulfilled the four roles of co-devlopers: as colleagues in a professional learning community, as external facilitators and field-based developers in schools, as contributors to applied research, and as disseminators of information.

- Co-developers external to the school unit or district were able to serve as catalysts for interest and call to action; co-developers internal to the school unit or district had some formal authority that helped support follow-up activities and the allocation of resources.

- We found that individuals with substantial knowledge, skills, and experience in school improvement are needed to launch and sustain the effort of transforming schools into PLCs. Strong credentials in that regard are a prerequisite for successfully fulfilling the roles. Additionally, these individuals must be willing learners as each co-developer had much to learn—both about PLCs and about participating in action research.

Training to Prepare Co-Developers

PLC conferences were designed to foster supportive relationships among co-developers so that they could experience on a firsthand basis the benefits of learning communities, and so they might fully contribute to the emerging understanding of the creation and function of professional learning communities.

- The structure of the CCCII project and the schedule of meetings provided critical preparation for co-developers as they selected and engaged schools in the project. The forming of a PLC among co-developers was an important prerequisite for accomplishing the work in schools.
- The content of the training was a "best guess" at the time. If another co-developer group were formed today, some topics would be dropped and others added. Topics might also take on a general sequence; some topics have been found to be more important at earlier stages of work with the school than others.
- Interim communications between SEDL staff and the co-developers was important in keeping everyone focused and in collecting data about the schools and the PLC development process. As future projects are planned, increasing the frequency of contacts and formalizing more of the reports should be considered. Additionally, an attempt should be made to utilize technology to support these contacts through such tools as on-line surveys, telephone interviews, e-mail reports, and chat room opportunities.

The Importance of Support

The "grand idea" will not happen without support from within the system in which the school is located.

- The importance of district-level support for developing PLCs within schools is critical. In many of the PLC sites for the CCCII project, the school activities stalled, stopped, or were never initiated because of actions or inactions at the district level. Securing board of education and superintendent advocacy and support are necessary conditions to make the implementation processes more likely to occur.

- Time for collaboration and learning continues to be a crucial element. While there is really nothing new in this lesson learned, the PLC project is yet another example that reinforces the understanding that change is a process, not an event. Those wanting to create and sustain PLCs in their schools and districts must be committed to long-term and in-depth change, and that requires time.

CONCLUSION

At the beginning of the project, 30 individuals gathered to meet one another and learn about PLCs. They committed themelves collectively and individually to creating a community of professional learners among themselves and within a variety of schools. Each of these individuals was an accomplished educator with a commitment to school renewal measured by their willingness to engage in such a challenge.

The staff at SEDL sought to provide the co-developers with a conceptual framework that would serve them—and others—in creating significant positive change in the nation's schools. The following six chapters provide details about what happened in some of the schools where co-developers worked to establish PLCs as a way to improve teacher and student learning. While we still have much to learn and accomplish, we believe we have all—together—made a strong start.

CHAPTER 8

Two Professional Learning Communities: Tales from the Field

Kristine Kiefer Hipp and Jane Bumpers Huffman

This chapter recounts the stories of two schools that were trying to become professional learning communities. The authors of this chapter were co-developers at the schools—Northland Elementary School and Foxdale Middle School. Each of these schools had to some degree, independently and without naming them as such, incorporated PLC principles into their organizational structure prior to joining the Creating Communities of Continuous Inquiry and Improvement project. CCCII provided these schools a focus for continuing improvement efforts, and a means of assessing progress and identifying stumbling blocks in those efforts. In the context of this chapter, the five dimensions of a PLC also serve as a framework to interpret actions and structures at these schools over the course of this study. Such interpretation provides examples of the way in which personality and relationships—both individual and at the organizational level—influence strategies and insight into the ways that PLC practices can develop at a school.

NORTHLAND ELEMENTARY

Northland Elementary is located in a southern city with a population of 90,000, which boasts two universities, serves as a central service center for the northern part of the state, and lies within 30 miles of two major cities. Northland was built in 1973 and operates with an alternative calendar that serves 525 K–5 students year-round. Northland's student community is 50% Hispanic, 38% white, 11% African American, and 2% other ethnicities. Students' families are mostly low-income semiskilled and unskilled laborers. Most of the parents have acquired, but not continued beyond, a high school diploma.

Forty-two certified staff serve the school, along with 10 paraprofessionals and 10 support personnel. Sixteen percent of the staff are male, and 84% are female. With regard to race, 61% of the staff are white, 30% are Hispanic, and 9% are African American. Twenty-one percent of the staff have master's degrees. Twenty-two staff members have 10 years' or less teaching experience, and 15 are in their first or second year of teaching. Twelve teachers have taught at Northland for more than 11 years.

Shared Leadership and Collective Learning Are a Way of Life at Northland

Northland's journey toward school improvement began in the early 1990s, when the Campus Leadership Team initiated a process to determine a unifying instructional focus for the school. After reviewing several programs and philosophies, the faculty agreed to adopt Learning Styles as the instructional focus for the school—a clear episode of shared leadership, vision, and collective learning. By using learning styles, the faculty could individualize instruction for the students, based on their learning preferences. Northland adopted other practices during the early 1990s that fit easily within the PLC dimensions, and thus formed an experiential base on which to purposefully build PLC practices.

An example of collective learning occurred during the 1992–1993 school year, when the faculty studied the possibility of a year-round school. A task force was formed and study groups explored the research. The district approved a pilot for implementation of an extended calendar for Northland. A proposal was developed in 1993 by the leadership team and meetings were held with faculty and parents to get feedback and suggestions. In July 1994, the school started its first year on the new alternative calendar. In subsequent years, several reviews of the program were conducted; these reviews culminated in a 1997 school board decision to adopt the alternative calendar as a regular schedule for Northland. This successful, student-centered initiative contributed to a feeling of empowerment for faculty and staff. Since then, the Campus Leadership Team has continued to provide effective shared leadership in major decisions about budgeting, scheduling, and staff development.

The CCCII project fit easily into Northland's existing structure of review and reform. The co-developer first gained central office approval and encouragement. Next, she contacted the principal and shared several phone and in-person conversations. The principal then scheduled a meeting with the Campus Leadership Team where the project was again introduced, discussed, and approved.

During the initial stages of the project, the principal and Campus Leadership Team were interested and accepting of the PLC model. They valued the information and were open to consider how the learning community concept could be incorporated into their school culture. However, they were clear that the decision to participate needed to involve all staff. The co-developer was invited to the faculty meeting to present information and answer questions about the PLC. The faculty embraced the idea and agreed to join the project.

An important issue for the staff was that they work closely, yet slowly. The principal was also concerned that the staff might feel like CCCII was being imposed upon them. Therefore, the principal and the co-developer acknowledged the values and culture of the school, and assured the staff that the operating procedures would not initially be disrupted. The staff projected a need to study information and to determine what was best for their students. They were open to change, but needed to understand how working together as a PLC would benefit their students in the classroom.

Assessing the Five Dimensions

In 1998, the first year of the SEDL project, administration and review of SEDL's *School Professional Staff as a Learning Community* survey (Hord, 1996) led the Northland staff to reconsider their focus and strategies. Organized around the five dimensions, the PLC questionnaire helped the staff identify two areas of concern: shared personal practice and shared values and vision. The staff requested more time to observe each other's classes in order to develop shared personal practice and increase individual and organizational capacity. They also wanted to visit other schools as needed. The principal offered support and substitutes to cover their classes. The staff also wanted to revisit the vision in order to identify what was needed to achieve high-quality learning experiences for all students.

Revisiting the vision, especially the focus on student learning, led to a faculty-initiated Saturday School, organized to provide students with more time to study, and to assist them in developing knowledge and skills for the state-mandated student achievement test. A committee of teachers designed the structure, curriculum, and instructional strategies, and staffed the four Saturday mornings. In the second year, this program resulted in student improvement on the state test. Perhaps more importantly, the teachers were further empowered by the sense of accomplishment gained in their efforts to meet student needs.

The Learning Styles program provided opportunities for Northland staff to develop and refine supportive conditions, both organizational and structural. Examples include support groups, staff development opportunities, and the use of resource materials. The Children at Risk Educational

(C.A.R.E.) Team was developed to provide support for individual teachers who encounter students that face learning problems. Since the adoption of Learning Styles as the school's instructional focus, there have been fewer students referred or identified for special education.

Teachers at Northland felt they had the opportunity to request support for materials, conference attendance, or other resource needs. They viewed administrators as trustworthy and sensitive to their needs. Faculty and Campus Leadership Team meetings were marked by a climate of genuine concern and respect indicative of a close family. Faculty and administrators often offered words of appreciation, encouragement, and congratulations to each other—another example of personal supportive conditions.

In 1999, after the co-developer and the project lead teacher attended a SEDL conference, the lead teacher proposed a more formal teacher induction program for the new teachers as a means of communicating and reinforcing school vision. The proposal was accepted and the teacher took responsibility for the plan. This program provided a clearer understanding by the new teachers of Northland's vision, policies, and procedures. In addition, a faculty retreat held at the beginning of the school year helped to incorporate new faculty into the school community, and to energize the entire faculty for the coming year.

Using PLC Dimensions for Planning

At the beginning of the 1999–2000 school year, the entire staff were again asked how they had been using the PLC dimensions, and what they would like to do this year in relation to the project. The teachers identified three major areas of concern. First, they wanted early release days so they could conduct long-range planning. Second, they wanted more time to plan and learn in teams on a weekly basis. Third, they again wanted to visit each other's classes and provide one another feedback. These areas defined the focus for the year. They were placed on the agenda for the leadership team and were implemented.

Faculty want more opportunities during the school day to meet in grade-level teams for long-range planning. A proposal for three early release days for common planning was discussed. This effort provided time for Northland faculty to continue their efforts in strengthening communication and curriculum alignment.

Northland's staff identified shared personal practice twice as an area they were interested in pursuing. The staff responded as such to the PLC questionnaire in 1998 and, as a faculty, also discussed this issue in 1999. Although they have recognized the potential benefits of sharing practice, they have not been actively engaged or supported to accomplish this. While informal discussions of classroom strategies and student work crop up at meetings and during tutoring time after school, there is no systematic way to share information. The staff needs to discover alternative ways to share practice and personal practical knowledge (Edwards, Butler, Hill, & Russell, 1997). As the culture of collaborative learning grows, strategies must also develop that allow this practice to occur.

Progress over the past years has been highly encouraging. Northland's faculty has energetically adapted the PLC dimensions in their quest to best serve students. The faculty is truly committed to providing the best program for their students as they work to achieve their motto, "Northland School—a great place to grow." The faculty continues to move slowly yet surely toward that end.

FOXDALE MIDDLE SCHOOL

Foxdale Middle School is located in a middle-income suburban district in the Midwest. The school serves 522 students in grades 5–8. Approximately 75% of the students are white, 19% are African American, 5% are Asian, and 1% are Hispanic. Twelve percent of these students are defined as economically disadvantaged based on eligibility for the free and reduced lunch program. Ten percent of the students are bused from outside the school attendance area. Data collected on parents indicate that approximately 40% are professionals, 20% hold technical positions, and 40% hold skilled or semiskilled labor jobs.

There are 51 professional staff members at Foxdale—30 females and 21 males, predominantly white. The school has a highly educated, committed faculty, with 82% having a master's degree. They are a "seasoned" staff, with 37 teachers having more than 15 years' experience, 11 with 6 to 15 years experience, and only three teachers with less than 5 years of experience. The attendance rate for students is approximately 95%. No student dropouts are documented, yet a significant number of behavioral referrals occur each year.

Foxdale Overcomes Concerns

The Foxdale Middle School principal actively pursued the challenging opportunity of creating a PLC. By the time the co-developer visited the school, the principal had already met with the superintendent to share information and determine his impressions. He considered the opportunity intriguing and congruent with the school district's vision. He wholeheartedly supported the effort despite two potential barriers that could hinder participation. First, a majority of teachers would be retiring within the following 5 years, and most teachers were predictably skeptical, as they had been involved in multiple innovations that seemed to have passed with the wind. Second, despite their significant educational experience, these teachers continue to face major challenges in the district, including failed referendums, steadily decreasing test scores, declining enrollment, and morale issues resulting from public criticism.

As at Northland, the Foxdale principal scheduled a meeting with the school's leadership team. Two meetings occurred. The first was rather brief and did not include the entire leadership team. When more information was requested, a dinner meeting was scheduled to further discuss the project with all members of the team. The overview of the SEDL project stimulated enthusiasm and hope for change amid a climate of distrust that had evolved from a growing lack of confidence from parents and community members. By the meeting's end, the team generated a strategy to introduce the project at the next staff meeting.

The co-developer presented the project at an all-school faculty meeting, with assistance from the head union negotiator—an influential staff member from the leadership team. Before they broke into small groups to discuss potential participation in the project, this teacher asked the staff to reflect on the following question: "Are you satisfied with the way things are in the school and district, and if not, are you open to try something new?" The staff discussed issues of morale and raised two major concerns: overload and finding time to learn together.

The co-developer addressed the fear of overload by maintaining that the project would not be an add-on, but instead would be integrated into current school initiatives. Using "Views of an Organization" (Senge, Kleiner, Roberts, Ross, & Smith, 1994) as an example, she helped staff to see the benefits of participating in a project that would promote a shared vision and more effective use of time. The Views of an Organization model offers three descriptions of organizations, in order of least to most desirable: not empowered and unfocused, empowered and unfocused, or empowered and focused. As is typical, Foxdale staff viewed their organization as reflecting the middle scenario, and were stimulated by Senge's description to work to achieve the ideal, empowered and focused. Moreover, to tackle the issue of time, it was suggested that the union negotiator and principal develop a plan of adding time to the school day in order to garner two "banking" days that could be devoted to the effort. This was not a final solution to the problem, but it was a beginning.

A subsequent meeting with the superintendent provided the opportunity for an exchange of ideas regarding the time issue and a shared sense of focus. As a result, Foxdale's teachers submitted a formal proposal to the teacher's union, in which they advocated adding 5 minutes to the start of each school day in order to "bank time" to engage in meaningful dialogue about student learning. This proposal affected busing, students, parents, and teachers in three schools. It required trust and belief in those advocating the change.

The district teachers sensed the commitment of their colleagues and voted in favor of the "banked time" proposal. The next and possibly greatest challenge was in the area of transportation. The principal rode every bus route and met with every bus driver to assure the feasibility of the plan. In turn, the teachers and school board approved the proposal. This response was viewed by the project's lead teacher as "the most important step forward in showing the trust building that we really needed to get going for the staff, because trust is the first level at getting to a professional learning community."

Collective Learning Is Key

As with Northland, Foxdale embodies a staff that is committed to student academic success. Unlike Northland, Foxdale has never engaged in a formal visioning exercise; instead, the principal's focus on student learning and well-being sets the course for school improvement efforts. Prior to the 1999–2000 school year, the school's focus involved a standards project. A needs assessment, related to the standards project, was conducted and staff requested more time to share, learn from one another, and focus their time and effort more effectively. These results aligned with the needs identified from the PLC questionnaire that was completed in May 1998. As at Northland, questionnaire results suggested a need to focus on collective learning and shared personal practice. The five components of a professional learning community provided direction for this process and involved staff in widespread collaborative activities.

As soon as the project began in the fall of 1998, the principal and teachers began to engage in collective learning more purposefully. As the school year emerged, teachers exhibited greater trust in one another as they more readily shared their opinions, beliefs, and values with less fear of repercussion. The more they seemed to reveal, the closer they became.

The standards project provided teachers with multiple days of training, offering many options, to address standards, benchmarks, and appropriate assessments. One of the two monthly staff meetings and all professional development days during the 1999–2000 school year were reserved for this effort. One teacher indicated, "We aren't teaching in a vacuum, but in a cohesive team environment, sharing lessons, successes and failures, and learning from each other." Teachers were being held accountable for what they were teaching and the effects on students. The five dimensions of a PLC, offering a common language and direction, continued to fuel this effort.

As the years progressed, banked time, staff meetings, and other professional days have changed. Initially, trust and team-building activities, now perceivably rare, provoke memories that staff continue to hunger for. These included simple activities with transforming results, such as "True Colors," in which staff assessed their preferred styles, and learned to appreciate all styles of learning. This allowed them to look deeper into both the needs and strengths of their existing teams. The staff scheduled an evening retreat, a "jazz" weekend in Chicago, pancake breakfasts, and a chili luncheon, just to name a few of the many activities designed to build relationships. On a more substantive level, at each planned breakfast and banked day, specific staff were recognized with the famed "Eddy Awards," an activity whereby each staff member's unique contribution was honored by year's end.

However, with a greater focus on developing instructional units aligned to standards and benchmarks, the tenor changed, and began to focus almost exclusively on student learning. Relationship and culture building took a backseat. During the second year, the staff seemed to move away from efforts supporting the human side of change. Life at Foxdale became almost too serious; the activities that ignited their enthusiasm and recognized their efforts appeared lost. As staff forged new ground, assumed new responsibilities, and reconfigured new teams, they worked to restore balance.

Awareness of the "implementation dip" is needed as faculty and facilitators plan for the future. Initiatives being implemented often mirror this dip, which in reality is a series of setbacks that tend to hinder progress. These setbacks are often due to a lack of resources and technical assistance, which cause frustration, anxiety, and a sense of hopelessness. Staffs that prevail through these uncertain times can potentially embed the change intended into the culture of the school. Dips in implementation are predictable; they can either destroy or reenergize the spirit for change (Fullan & Stiegelbauer, 1991).

During the 1998–1999 school year, a small group of teachers took a course based on Charlotte Danielson's (1996) *Enhancing Professional Practice: A Framework for Teaching*. Out of this experience, they created a document that was used in place of the school's standard teacher evaluation system. This document was required for new staff and utilized by others upon request. One component is an exchange of information through a process similar to peer coaching. Where trust existed, some teams already engaged in offering informal feedback.

Foxdale teachers demonstrated an unwavering commitment to student learning and collective inquiry. The current focus on professional teaching standards at Foxdale has united the school in a common purpose. The dimensions of a PLC offer a common language and drive existing efforts. There was a renewed sense of energy and hope that teachers could make a positive difference in the lives of their students, if provided continual support and encouragement. Experiences over the past years revealed that many teachers sensed a significant difference in the school climate, and that relationships changed. Collaboration and risk-taking gradually replaced isolation and fear. The school's mission, "Preparing Today's Students for Tomorrow's World," became a purpose with substance.

USING THE PLC MODEL TO INTERPRET SCHOOL ACTIONS

In both Northland and Foxdale, the five PLC dimensions promoted a common language among school staff that were engaged in this project. The dimensions provided focus and consistency across all school efforts, and now provide a method of interpreting actions.

Shared and Supportive Leadership

The principals in both schools shared decision-making and nurtured leadership development among their staffs. Prior to the CCCII project, these schools established school leadership teams through which most decisions were made, including the decision to join SEDL's effort. Membership on the team changed from year to year, either by election or rotation. There tended to be a three-tiered process with the leadership team in the middle. The principal made some decisions, while those involving implementation by staff were generally made with input from a greater number of staff. It was often the leadership team's responsibility to represent the teachers' views and also take information back to the teachers by sharing or eliciting suggestions for decisions.

Both leadership teams met regularly, a critical element in informing and empowering members. They were often faced with a view of the larger picture, a picture difficult for teachers to see within the four walls of a classroom. Each person was expected to speak up and be represented, and to actively participate in the decision-making and collective learning in his or her school. When roles and responsibilities shifted and teachers were engaged in decision-making, there existed varying degrees of comfort. Some embraced opportunities for leadership, while others preferred to be told what to do.

The staff at both schools believed that the collaborative leadership team offered a true opportunity for representative leadership. A sense of responsibility—both to teachers and to the leadership teams—was evident in the operation of these systems.

Faculty at these two schools also engaged in professional growth activities outside of school, and returned to facilitate collegial activities. Moreover, teachers served as committee chairpersons and facilitated decisions where all voices were heard and no one person, including the principal, had more power than any single member.

Shared Values and Vision

At Northland, involvement in CCCII provided the opportunity for the staff and leadership to focus again on the school's vision. Administration of the PLC questionnaire resulted in rich discussion and the development of shared concerns and struggles. Through this interchange of ideas, the faculty expressed their assumptions about school improvement as well as their perceived needs for the students. This ongoing conversation allowed the staff to be more direct in their overall efforts and teaching strategies targeted toward high-quality learning experiences for *all* students. One example of this was the after-school tutoring program that assisted students who needed extra help. This effort served to energize and unify the staff as they assisted the students and each other in providing successful opportunities and outcomes for students.

As previously mentioned, Foxdale's vision, expressed by the principal to the staff, focused on student learning and well-being. The vision complemented the district's mission statement, "to prepare our children to be lifelong learners and to succeed in tomorrow's world." In order to connect the SEDL project to the district's mission, which visibly adorns the hallways of the school and is verbalized upon demand by Foxdale's staff, a model was created that captured the heart of school efforts.

As Foxdale staff engaged in various initiatives, a common language emerged that encouraged a focus on this vision in practice. For instance, the Standards project rallied all staff to develop units incorporating critical reasoning skills and knowledge-construction strategies. Some teachers were further along than others, but all staff were held accountable for improving instructional methods for student gains.

Collective Learning and Application

Faculty at both Northland and Foxdale engaged in similar activities. Both scheduled staff-led book studies outside of the defined school day. These book studies were well attended and provided opportunities for staff to initiate and sustain growth and professional development on their terms, related to school goals and the specific needs of their students. Various teachers assumed the role of facilitator. They also focused on classroom management skills and on the at-risk learner.

Coincidentally, both schools sent an administrator and teachers to a national workshop on the at-risk learner. Staff returned to their schools to share what they had learned and to serve as resources. Nonetheless, although faculty meetings involved more collective learning, peer learning predominantly existed in small groups (teams, grade levels, and committees) rather than as a whole school.

Such projects as Northland's Learning Styles and Foxdale's standards effort have assisted staff at both schools in targeting learning and reducing the fragmentation and isolation normally experienced by staff. Staff meetings became more interactive; collaborative teams worked together to design instructional strategies for students. Nonetheless, the barrier of time still looms over both schools, as current schedules continue to hinder opportunity.

Supportive Conditions

The issue of time was significant for staff at both schools. It was critical as teachers grappled with whole-school issues, made decisions in line with the schools' visions, learned collectively, and shared practice. Northland staff insisted that efforts progress slowly and acknowledge the culture of the school; Foxdale's staff were adamant against tackling "one more thing." At each school, the SEDL project integrated efforts and thereby strengthened already existing initiatives.

In addition, the principals and staff at Northland and Foxdale were instrumental in restructuring the school day. Northland's efforts involved the implementation of a "year-round school" that provided more time for staff to interact collaboratively and exchange effective practices. By adding 5 minutes to the start of each school day, Foxdale's staff acquired two "banking days" beyond the district scheduled staff development days, which provided a significant amount of time for unit writing, sharing of practice, and coaching in incorporating critical reasoning skills and knowledge construction strategies into integrated team units. The time allotted never seemed to be enough, yet there was a visible commitment to seeking support for faculty learning.

The principals at both schools have focused on trust as a critical factor in the creation of their PLCs. Shared decision-making processes and flattened hierarchical structures encouraged shared leadership and empowerment of both faculties. For the most part, due to significant restructuring of teams, trust began to emerge despite Foxdale's peaks and valleys. Just when the staff were beginning to openly share and become comfortable with one another, the teams were reconfigured and new relationships were forged. Nonetheless, as at Northland, there was a powerful sense of compassion and caring likened to a family, and a strong value of continuous learning. At both schools, staff were reinforced by administrators and peers for any initiative they took as it related to increasing student learning and well-being.

Shared Personal Practice

Hord (1997a) viewed shared personal practice as including classroom observations and feedback by teachers, which is similar to the concept of peer coaching. Results from the PLC questionnaire across the 22 schools reported this dimension to be that which was least applied. Considering this narrow view of shared personal practice, it is unlikely in the near future that many schools will be able to create structures that allow for most of its staff to engage in these activities within the school day.

At Northland, staff requested substitutes to cover classes so that observations could be made. At Foxdale, teachers in the arts, in special education, and in the Alternative Program for at-risk students are, at times, set up to work in the same room together. However, under the current K–12 structure, such shared practice occurred on infrequent and irregular bases. Schools need to embed the sharing of practice as an ongoing staff development activity that occurs throughout the school day.

Aside from observations and coaching, other activities were evident in both schools that worked in tandem with those cited in collective learning. Whether focusing on learning styles or writing units incorporating standards, benchmarks, and appropriate assessment measures, teachers working collaboratively are sharing their personal practical knowledge and skills (Edwards et al., 1997).

FINAL THOUGHTS

This chapter showed how the dimensions of professional learning communities can assist schools already engaged in school improvement efforts by focusing those efforts, and by providing a means of assessing progress.

In addition, the PLC dimensions provide an organizational scheme that can facilitate thinking about change and interpreting changes. Even efforts begun or undertaken with no knowledge of professional learning communities can be organized within the PLC framework, and placed on a continuum of PLC activities. Such interpretation provides energy and direction for the ongoing task of sustaining school improvement.

CHAPTER 9

Change Diaries: Parallel Perspectives on School Change

Richela Chapman and Dawn Watson

Driving down a lonely West Texas highway, the co-developer watched a sleepy little town surrounded by orchards appear on the horizon. In addition to a peanut plant, the school district was a major employer in this area, organized into four campuses: primary, intermediate, middle, and high school. Both town and district had a long history of maintaining the status quo. This year the school district would be receiving a District Effectiveness and Compliance (DEC) visit from the Texas Education Agency. Student achievement data, documentation on special programs, and campus/district improvement plans would be reviewed. This was perceived as a threat, and people were nervous about being "under the microscope."

An experienced school change agent with a keen eye toward "readiness for change" in schools, the co-developer was in the process of selecting a school to participate in SEDL's Creating Communities of Continuous Inquiry and Improvement project. To the co-developer, Thomas Jefferson Elementary School seemed a promising place to begin. From the diaries/ journals of the two educational leaders—the co-developer and the principal—we will follow the Jefferson story.

INTRODUCTIONS

The Co-Developer: Planting a Seed for Change

When I arrived for my first appointment with the principal, a child was sitting on the principal's lap, crying. She was patting, hugging, and reassuring him while asking questions softly in his ear. He was nodding and sobbing. When he quieted, she asked if he was ready to return to his room. He nodded and she helped him off her lap before turning her attention to me. Seeing that she put children first made me think that she might be a good partner in the SEDL project.

I introduced myself as Title I contact for the district and asked if I could be of service to her in their upcoming DEC visit. Title I provides federal funding for disadvantaged children, either through Targeted Assistance Programs, which serve children identified as most in need, or Schoolwide Programs, which upgrade the entire educational program at the school. As the district specialist, I provided technical assistance in planning, applying for funding, budgeting, monitoring progress, and accessing resources.

The principal was open to assistance from me, and asked me to review her campus plan. We visited about the Title I Targeted Assistance Program at Jefferson, which consisted of a computerized reading and math lab. The principal was concerned about children sitting in front of computers and being pulled out of their regular classes. I asked if she had done a longitudinal study on the progress of these students. She hesitated then said, "No, I haven't." I planted a seed for change.

The Principal: New to Elementary School

Elementary school—I had no idea what to do in an elementary school. I had been principal of an alternative education program that served at-risk high school students from 12 neighboring districts. During my 2 years in alternative education, I learned how to find resources, design curriculum to meet students' needs, and select personnel. Not sure what was ahead, but loving new challenges, I took on the challenge of coming to Jefferson Elementary.

At the time, I did not know that my inexperience in elementary schools would actually help our school change and improve. After reflecting on our 3 years of growth, I believe my lack of experience contributed to shared leadership at the school. Asking questions and gaining input from my staff gave them ownership of the school and created opportunities for collaborative decision-making.

Our DEC visit was a blessing in disguise, an external factor that helped us reform programs and make much-needed changes. By studying the DEC indicators, the staff saw that changes in special programs such as English as a Second Language, Gifted/Talented Education, Migrant Education, Special Education, and Title I were needed to benefit our children.

THE INTERACTIONS OF THE CO-DEVELOPER AND PRINCIPAL

The Co-Developer: Watering the Seed for Change

I set out to find a change-ready site as soon as I learned of my selection by SEDL as a co-developer in the CCCII project. I mentally scanned all the districts I served to identify possible sites. I asked myself questions such as, "Do I know any schools facing a crisis? What schools are representative of the diversity of students in our state? Would any of the schools with which I work welcome this opportunity? Which superintendents exhibit leadership qualities and trust my leadership capabilities? Are any of these schools close to my office at the regional education service center?"

I sensed a strong readiness for change and openness for learning in the principal of Jefferson Elementary. That primary campus served approximately 200 PK–third grade students with a mobility rate of 30%. Ethnic distribution on the campus was 17% African American, 37% Hispanic, and 46% white; 11% were classified as limited English proficient, and 68% were economically disadvantaged. With leadership and diversity, I felt this was an excellent site for the SEDL project.

I explained the nature of the project to the principal in February 1998. Wanting to provide choice and opportunity, I asked, "Do you think you'd be interested in participating?" With bright eyes and animated face, she replied, "We want to. Please choose us!" She perched on the edge of her chair, her body language exuding enthusiasm. It was absolutely delightful to observe such a strong interest, coupled with a positive attitude toward continuous learning.

As we visited, I suggested that moving from Title I targeted assistance to a schoolwide program could help the school improve. She agreed, confessing that there were many barriers to change among the faculty. I watered the seed for change.

The Principal: Push for Inclusion

The co-developer's ability to ask questions and lead was remarkable. I am sure our first meeting revealed to her that I had a lot to learn. I did not even know what a Title I program was, or that we needed to change it. I did know children could not learn to read by sitting in front of a computer with no adult instruction. The co-developer suggested I do a study of identified Title I students to track their progress. The children were not improving. However, I knew I could not just go in and tell my teachers, "No one is learning and we have to change." I wanted change to be their idea.

Our Title I targeted assistance computer lab program contract was up for renewal. I used this opportunity to call a staff meeting. At the meeting, the entire staff was given the results of the longitudinal study. It showed our students weren't improving in the lab, the cost of maintaining the lab, and how our Title I funds could be spent if we chose to go from targeted assistance to schoolwide. In fairness, I asked the computer lab's representative to "sell" their math and reading program to the teachers.

Once the dust settled, only the two Title I targeted assistance program teachers voted to keep the program. Other faculty wanted a school-wide program. Change was scary, but this opened the door to change the way we did business. These two teachers were reassigned to regular classrooms. By using our federal funds differently, we were able to place a paraprofessional at each grade level, and purchase a supplementary reading program. People working directly with children made decisions in the best interest of children. I loved it.

We began our push for total inclusion. We wanted to eliminate pull-out programs for our children. The retirement of the district Gifted and Talented (G/T) teacher in May gave us leverage to convince the board to train our teachers to serve G/T students in the classroom. To be certified, all teachers needed 30 hours of training in G/T strategies. We were fortunate that our co-developer's master's degree was in gifted and talented education. She trained the entire teaching staff that summer.

The Co-Developer: Title I Decision

The faculty examined the data, discussed how they could best utilize their federal funds, and voted not to renew the Title I computer lab contract. This was a critical incident for them, as this year of planning enabled them to restructure the school utilizing Title I funds to assist all the children, not just a targeted few.

This dynamic principal wanted good things for her students and exhibited keen interest in this project as well as good follow-through after each of our conversations. My next step was to visit with the superintendent regarding the school's participation in the project. Being a laissez-faire leader, he said, "Whatever she wants to do."

My next mission was to get in the door with the faculty, build trust, and meet their needs. My goal was to build community by helping the school accomplish *its* goals. The SEDL project would be my vehicle. My destination was increased student achievement, school improvement, and people empowerment. My motto became, "Do whatever it takes."

I offered to provide the 30 hours of professional development in the nature and needs of gifted/talented learners, curriculum, and assessment. A faculty meeting was scheduled to assess needs and set a date for the professional development. The principal arranged with the superintendent and school board for teachers to receive a summer professional development stipend. This was a wonderful opportunity for me to build trust and rapport with the faculty.

We were well on our way to establishing a strong partnership. At our next meeting we discussed roles in implementing CCCII. As external change agent, I provided support through data analysis and campus improvement planning, located funding for programs they wanted to implement, and assisted in leveraging resources.

As internal change agent at the campus, the principal supplied needed data, facilitated faculty growth in the five dimensions of professional learning communities, provided time, leveraged resources from the district, and attended SEDL meetings in Austin. She appointed Terry Monroe as her "teacher leader" and partner in CCCII. As resource teacher at the campus, Terry worked with special needs children, had access to teachers' classrooms, and met regularly with grade-level teams to plan for students' needs. Terry networked with the faculty and provided insight into the implementation of the five dimensions of a professional learning community (see Chapter 2).

The Principal: Appointing a Teacher Leader

I chose Terry Monroe as our teacher leader because, as our content mastery teacher, she worked with all the teachers. Terry monitored the progress of resource students who could have been placed in a special education resource room, but who also could master regular content with support. To this end, she worked with the content teachers during their planning time and during the academic time. In this way, Terry helped meet the children's needs, plus she acted as my barometer for school climate. Terry was able to provide insight into how everyone really felt about our changes, and feedback on the attitude of the staff from their perspective.

CRITICAL INCIDENTS IN PLC DEVELOPMENT

Critical incidents are those happenings or activities, either large or small, that appear to significantly alter the course of events in a change effort. In the following excerpts from their diaries, the two change agents discuss such events.

The Co-Developer: The First Critical Incidents

The first critical incident in school improvement occurred when the faculty chose to discontinue the school's Title I Targeted Assistance Program, a computer-based pullout program, to become a Title I Schoolwide Program. The second was when I shared *Best Practice: New Standards for Teaching and Learning in America's Schools* (Zemelman, Daniels, & Hyde, 1998) with the principal. She thought it would move her staff along in school improvement and ordered copies for faculty study. When the books arrived, they were distributed to faculty with instructions to read Chapter 1 and to be prepared to discuss it at the next faculty meeting. Each month this book provided the faculty with topics that helped them examine what and how they taught children. It also provided a conduit for changes in curriculum and opened the way for dialoguing and building trust among staff.

The Principal: Our First Step in Collective Learning

Our co-developer supplied information, materials, and resources. She shared a book called *Best Practice: New Standards for Teaching and Learning in America's Schools* (Zemelman, Daniels, & Hyde, 1998). It described the multisensory learning experiences I wanted our students to experience.

Book study was our first step in collective learning—one of the five PLC dimensions. We actively discussed what we were doing right in instruction, what was not good instruction, and what we needed to change. We read a chapter each month and met after school as a faculty—until we were talked out. After the first few chapters, I asked if they wanted to continue and all felt the book was worth finishing. Not only were they learning new ideas, but saw that they already utilized many good practices. This really built confidence in their teaching strategies. Eventually the staff took responsibility for the book study. I no longer facilitated the discussions, indicating a growth in teacher leadership and empowerment.

We believed the textbooks that we were using were not helping our students meet the state's standards. To begin our exploration of textbook options, I arranged for my teachers to visit other primary schools. After researching several math programs, we met as a faculty to decide which one to adopt. I called several publishers and asked them to come give a "sales pitch" to the entire faculty. The teachers had never had a textbook representative speak to them and they did not look forward to staying after school and listening to a salesperson. However, this forced the teachers to examine closely the material being offered. Afterward, we came to consensus regarding the supplementary text. We began working with the new math program one year prior to its inclusion on the state adoption list. We used this year to identify missing links in the math curriculum.

It is interesting to reflect that as much as they dreaded the textbook salespeople's first visit, the following year the grade-level teachers asked if we could have textbook representatives visit with them again. Several teachers formed a textbook committee to begin vertical alignment of our curriculum with our feeder campus.

The Co-Developer: Progress in Implementation

The principal, Terry, and I met to check Jefferson's progress in implementing the five dimensions of a professional learning community. More dialogue and feedback among staff was needed. We wanted to examine the state-mandated student achievement data and make changes in the campus plan based on improvements and needs. We needed to focus on summarization, inferences, and generalizations in reading instruction, and math problem-solving using solution strategies.

Chapter 3 of the *Best Practice* book (Zemelman, Daniels, & Hyde, 1998) addressed journal writing. The concept of "read my mind" was debated, and the lab was used for writing instruction. The principal remarked to the faculty that all she had seen in the lab was "fill in the blank." As the teachers thought about the lab and how it could be used to better assist students with the writing process, they began to ask questions of each other and answer each other's questions instead of relying on their principal to guide the discussion. This collective learning activity facilitated the development of teacher leadership on the campus.

The Principal: Observation as a Way to Grow

We determined the next growing experience for the teachers should be to observe one another. Earlier, I had asked the teachers to write the name of someone in the school whom they would like to observe. Observations were scheduled after Christmas. Upon seeing the schedule, though, many teachers protested. One told me she would go to beauty school before allowing anyone to watch her teach.

While everyone was reluctant about being observed, all the teachers were excited about being able to observe. A calendar was distributed. Everyone had access to the observation schedule. Substitutes were hired so that the teachers could spend a half day in observation. We were growing in collective learning.

The Co-Developer: At Year's End

Near the end of our first year in CCCII, the principal, Terry, and I visited regarding our progress in the five dimensions. As we planned our staff development calendar for the following year, we determined that the SEDL "mini-modules" on dialoguing and the process of giving feedback could be integrated. We wanted staff to learn the difference between two forms of conversation: *dialogue* and *discussion*. Dialogue was to be used to generate ideas without judgement, to foster collective meaning-making, and to help create shared understanding. Discussion, on the other hand, was used to allow the group to weigh options, to engage in rigorous critical thinking, and to make decisions. Small groups practiced dialogue using "Teacher Talk That Makes a Difference" by Garmston and Wellman (1999). Our first staff development day next year would be devoted to campus planning: evaluating and revising our campus plan, and analyzing student scores on the state-mandated criterion referenced test that provided us disaggregated student achievement data. The staff needed a 6-hour update in Gifted/Talented Education to remain certified.

PUSHING PLC DEVELOPMENT

The Principal: Something Is Missing

While the observation schedule forced teachers into each other's classrooms, not enough "critical" feedback on quality in student work was shared. For many teachers, this peer observation experience evoked their first real awareness that teachers are not individually self-employed but that they are part of a bigger system. Feedback was not focused on student learning but on personal compliments. Heightened awareness of their interdependency, both professional and personal, made many afraid of "stepping on toes."

Even though we had discontinued all "pullout" programs, I still felt there was something missing—something that could connect the academic content knowledge we had gained with all the professional knowledge about teaching we were learning. Making that connection would surely impact student learning.

At an inclusion conference in 1999, several teachers and I attended a workshop on brain compatible learning. During this workshop, the Tribes process (Gibbs, 1995) was described. Through cooperative learning strategies, the Tribes process helps schools create small student learning communities in a caring, supportive school environment. The next year at the conference, I took two more teachers to the same workshop. Our co-developer loaned me a copy of the book. A few copies were ordered so we would have a chance to decide whether or not Tribes was really what we wanted to implement. The faculty met several times to determine whether this would be worth the financial and time commitments. After negotiating with administration, a waiver allowed staff 3 days of in-service.

The Co-Developer: More Training

After the faculty finished *Best Practices*, the next significant event was professional development in Tribes. The principal located a trainer for Tribes and the School Board approved 3 waiver days so that her entire staff could attend. As it turned out, this training was another critical incident in their growth toward a professional learning community, as faculty learned how to work together for student learning.

The Principal: Tribes

We hired a Tribes trainer and went on a Tribes retreat on the first of September in 1999. During the retreat, our trainer facilitated the material in a way that demonstrated its use and developed community among the faculty. By using this process, the trainer stripped us of our roles, as we had currently conceptualized them.

> It is this intentional transfer of leadership in the midst of a positive and caring environment that makes the Tribes program different from other cooperative learning methods. This transfer, this calling forth, is the big secret to building self-worth and motivation among people. No matter what the age level, it gives a loud and clear message—you are capable people who can indeed manage yourselves and help each other! (Gibbs, 1995, p. 78)

This was it. This was the professional learning community we had been striving for—a community that focused on students and integrated the pieces. Following this training, I began to see the faculty coalescing as learners.

The Co-Developer: Data Analysis

We decided to review the state achievement data for the campus and district prior to the next staff development day. We designed an agenda and determined our roles. The in-service began with the faculty reviewing longitudinal data. In the past, the faculty had only looked at current-year data, and I felt that a broader perspective was needed. I had disaggregated the data by specific objective and grade level so that the teachers could easily see how the students were achieving as they moved through the system. I explained the state's Academic Excellence Indicator System (AEIS) report and showed them how to use the campus comparison group, district comparison group, and state data to gauge their own performance. After data review, teachers met to identify campus needs and resources. To revise the current plan, teachers met in grade-level teams to determine what was and was not working. Each grade level revised its section of the plan. Student achievement data determined the focus for the year.

The Principal: A First Examination of Data

The fall in-service was the first time teachers had ever *really* looked in depth at the state achievement test numbers and had longitudinal student achievement data explained to them. Our co-developer showed us how to read the AEIS report and explained comparison groups. Since Jefferson had always been the highest scoring campus in the district, the faculty had felt no pressure in the past to make improvements. The faculty used our high number of low socioeconomic students as an excuse for low achievement. It was noted that Hispanic males were not achieving as well as other groups in the school and suggested that the campus focus on strategies for that specific group. Teachers actively participated in setting reading and math achievement goals and objectives that addressed our areas for growth. Teachers agreed to attend staff development in these identified areas, such as summarization and problem solving. A staff development calendar was collaboratively designed and included in our campus plan.

MEASURES OF PROGRESS

The Co-Developer: Changed But Confused

To gauge our progress on becoming a PLC, we administered the SEDL Questionnaire, *School Professional Staff as Learning Community* (Hord, 1996). These perceptions were measured against perceptions from the same questionnaire administered early in the project. In addition, a staff member from SEDL joined me in November to interview a cross-section of the faculty. This was another means of measuring the school's growth as a professional learning community. Responses were recorded and tran-scribed, and were fairly consistent among the 12 teachers interviewed.

Faculty related that supportive and shared leadership prevailed on the campus. Faculty shared values and vision of all children being success-ful, and treasured their collective learning experiences. Reading *Best Prac-tices* (Zemelman, Daniels, & Hyde, 1998) was affirming and provided ways to think about new strategies. Tribes brought more communication and interaction among teachers. Faculty were more open to sharing and making decisions regarding instructional issues.

Surprisingly, faculty seemed confused regarding a common vision. It was my feeling that their vision was so embedded in the school culture that no one articulated the goal of "all children reading on grade level by the end of third grade." This overarching theme would be addressed.

Faculty needed to understand more about professional learning com-munities. A copy of a SEDL newsletter *Issues about Change*, "Professional Learning Communities: What Are They and Why Are They Important" (Hord, 1997b) was distributed. A carousel activity was utilized to compare the findings of research to their campus. This reinforced the five dimen-sions of PLCs and provided faculty-positive input regarding their own progress in becoming a professional learning community.

The Principal: TESA Training

In April, our co-developer Terry and I analyzed our PLC questionnaire and decided to approach teacher observations and feedback again. We decided to provide Teacher Expectations for Student Achievement (TESA) training. It is designed to strengthen equitable questioning strategies and provide opportunities for professional feedback. Teachers would learn how to interact more successfully with students. The program required teachers to attend five staff development sessions, observe one another, document strategies used, and give appropriate feedback to one another.

When this idea was presented to the faculty, you could have heard a pin drop. The fear was palpable and I could hear teachers thinking, "Why does she keep coming back to this?" After a period of silence, a veteran teacher stated she had been through the TESA training and felt that it had really helped her. Ultimately, the majority of teachers came to admit the benefits of the training. New leaders were emerging from the staff.

The Co-Developer: Contagious Leadership

In March 2000, the principal called me regarding an "awesome break-through"—another critical incident. The March 10 in-service day had been set aside for site visitations to other schools, but the third grade teachers asked if they could use this day to share strategies tested on the state achievement test with teachers in grades one and two, another marker for growth in teacher leadership on the campus.

For the purpose of collective learning the staff met regularly to discuss school issues, share information, and learn with and from one another. Addressed were student-centered issues such as the study group once per month on *Best Practices*, instructional practices, and influences on student learning. Classroom observations enabled teachers to learn from one another. Discussion focused on student learning, rather than on social issues.

The principal and the teachers maximized interaction through memos, an information board, and whole-school faculty meetings where issues were discussed and whole-school decisions were made. Trust was built through study groups, collaboration, and joint decision-making.

The principal's openness to new ideas spread through the faculty, as she invited them to take ownership and responsibility for student learning. Her unwavering focus on children, which I spotted at our first meeting—more than 3 years ago—fueled the type of "contagious leadership" that allowed the school, and its children, to grow and continuously improve.

CHAPTER 10

One Principal's Story:
Building a Community of Inquiry

Brian Riedlinger

The analysis of school improvement classically describes schools that move or attempt to move from less than satisfactory performance to a more effective status. Studies of effective leadership typically describe actions taken by successful leaders, sometimes within the context of school improvement. There have been relatively few portraits of already successful schools and already successful principals who were dissatisfied with their accomplishments. This chapter depicts one such school and principal, examining the "good" school that undergoes systemic change and the "good" principal who seeks personal as well as professional transformation.

Influenced by the instructors and readings in a doctoral program in educational leadership, the principal came to view the positive reputation of the school as a sign of its untapped potential. This chapter describes several years of reading, reflection, and experimentation on the part of the principal; 2 years of active change at the school, during which the power structure was altered; and an ongoing period of reflection and implementation, during which the experiences of the past are mined for use in continuing school improvement efforts.

The term "good principal" is used with some hesitance since the principal described here is also the author, but it is the up-close, insider view of this process that gives the chapter the personal feel that is absent in some studies of school improvement.

The chapter provides an inside look at the successes and the shortcomings of this intentional upheaval within an effective school. Ultimately, this upheaval created a formal structure for shared decision-making. Deep structural change, or what some have termed "second order" change, enabled the stakeholders at the school (teachers, parents, community members, administrators and, in some cases, students) to transcend their individual frames of reference and confront problems as active, cooperative problem solvers.

A PERSONAL CHANGE

The structure and focus of this study require attention to the change that happened to me personally. My readings of education and change experts led me to reflect on themes that I previously had not considered: themes that embrace larger roles for both principals and schools. In much of my reading, principals were encouraged to act as leaders, incorporating into schools a vision of these organizations as instruments to bring about individual and societal change.

My personal readings during that same period included some Eastern philosophy, most significantly that of Lao Tzu. I began to see all that we do as a continuous process rather than a linear one. Applied to the change process, this vision asserts that no one period of the process is better or more important than any other. The adjustment in perspective was (and is) mysterious and gradual, but I was greatly affected.

My personal outlook on the role of the principal, power and authority, and the change process was transformed through reflection that was itself born of internal unrest. In retrospect, I see that my own "dis-ease" (the top-down style of most leaders at the time); the influence of Eastern philosophy; and the ideas of educational reformers such as Roland Barth, Thomas Sergiovanni, and Michael Fullan led me through five distinct periods of personal transformation as a school leader: blind compliance with the district's mission for the school, an extended period of dissonance, haphazard experimentation, intensive reflection, and finally an ongoing period I've come to call "action research." The results of my study break down into three distinct stages of school change: business as usual, empowerment-initiated conflict, and truly shared governance.

Accounts of the first three periods of my personal transformation were constructed through retrospective analysis. The later events, including the stages of school change, were documented through personal journaling, interviews, and focus groups held with teachers. The paradigm of leadership I developed on this journey is consistent with Blumberg and Greenfield's (1980) portrait of principals who "lead." Without my realizing it at the time, the school structure I established bears a strong resemblance to a professional learning community, as defined by Hord (1997a). I explored the connections between my findings, the research of Blumberg and Greenfield, and Hord's description of professional learning communities in schools.

FIVE PHASES OF PERSONAL TRANSFORMATION

Compliance

Lakehills Elementary School was opened in 1958 in an urban district in a large southern city and, almost from the start, was regarded as a premier school. Stability of the school administration, the location of the school in a middle- to upper-class neighborhood and an experienced staff all contributed to the positive reputation of Lakehills Elementary. In 1979, when Lakehills' principal retired after 19 years, there was no more coveted assignment in the district.

Armed with 7 years of teaching experience and a 5-year-old master's degree with certification in educational administration, I felt prepared to manage one of the district's leading elementary schools. My first impression was that the school was very good, but could be even better. The regional superintendent who supervised the school charged me with three tasks: increase enrollment, maintain good test scores, and increase the number of African American students from less than 20% to 50% of the enrollment. My immediate school focus was never in doubt.

Within the first 7 years, the enrollment more than doubled, test scores were higher than previously recorded, and the racial makeup of the school was consistently near 50% minority. Popularity of the school also soared, evidenced by lines of parents waiting for days to apply for the possibility of admission to the limited spaces afforded out-of-district students.

This period of compliance addressed immediate needs of the school and left little room for the untidy business of interpretation, discussion, disagreement, or input. This period also allowed a young, inexperienced principal to gain confidence in a directive and task-oriented atmosphere. Teachers as well as parents gained confidence in the principal's ability to "get things done." My initial compliance with district priorities helped to establish confidence, a positive working relationship, and a foundation upon which to build in later years.

The Beginning of Dissonance

After the first 7 years and the completion of the three previously mentioned charges outlined by the area superintendent, I sensed that only a new vision would move the already successful school forward, and that a personal change in style was necessary for my own professional growth. I recognized that the benevolent authoritarian style I employed would not encourage collaboration, and grew increasingly uncomfortable with that style of leadership. I sensed that I had to develop and employ a more facilitative style, but did not know how to make that style shift within myself and with the teaching staff. This period of dissonance, which is documented in much of the school change literature, provided the stimulus to look for a different way.

Haphazard Experimentation

Successful leaders are often described as changing, adapting, or realizing their personal style of collaborative leadership rather than simply managing tasks. In their case studies of extraordinary leadership, Kouzes and Posner's (1990) collaborative style of leadership is described as the most important change in effective organizations.

Over the next 2 to 3 years, I tried a number of different plans to create collaboration. I revamped the principal's advisory committee three times, giving it different names and using different methods of member selection. I instituted a parent-teacher advisory board, and held discussions of teaching styles, grade configurations, and other school issues. While many of these initiatives had positive results, they were undertaken as managerial or structural tasks, driven by my perception of what should be done. My control of the process was very important to me—and the greatest obstacle to real organizational change.

James Kotter (1991) clearly describes the difference between a leader and a manager. Kotter asserts that managers plan, budget, and set goals while leaders establish direction by developing a clear vision; managers establish organizations and structures while leaders align people with the vision and elicit cooperation; managers control, problem solve, set goals, and monitor, whereas leaders motivate and inspire by appealing to basic human needs and values. After my first 7 years, I realized that I was a manager, not a leader.

The collaborative traits I unconsciously desired differed from the control-oriented, managerial style I employed; collaborative traits required a high degree of professional as well as personal security. Many of the collaborative leadership characteristics felt natural to me; they were much the same as those I employed as a teacher, and would eventually describe my own administrative style. But these characteristics were not held in high regard by my instructors when I studied for my master's degree in administration in 1976; they were viewed as weaknesses by top-level administrators when I became a principal in 1979. These characteristics were seldom discussed, encouraged, or taught.

In addition, teachers at Lakehills Elementary were used to, and comfortable with, the congenial style that Barth (1990) describes. Congenial behavior is above all friendly; it is justified as "for the good of the school and students." Lakehills' teachers were uncomfortable with the rigorous collegial style that causes the whole school to work together for school improvement. In this collegial style, teachers skillfully confront one another, keeping an agreed-upon vision of the school foremost in their minds. This style is beneficial because the teachers are part of the problem-solving, solution-finding, and implementation-planning processes. At Lakehills, however, it was easier for teachers to let the principal make decisions with which they sometimes complied, and which they often criticized. Decisions held little value or commitment from the people who were charged with their implementation.

In short, this was a confusing time for me and for a staff that patiently tried to make sense of my unrest. But this period was, at the very least, action oriented. It demonstrated to teachers and parents that change was on the horizon, even if the shape and form were yet undetermined. It was shortly after that period that I enrolled in a doctoral program at a local university.

Reflection

As a part-time doctoral student and full-time administrator in the midst of a personal as well as professional change, the time spent working on my courses, acting as a principal, and reflecting upon both became important and valuable to the change about to take place. Sarason (1971) described school culture as the feel or ethos of a school, coupled with its behavioral regularities. Through my reading at the university, it became more apparent that I was unhappy with the culture of Lakehills Elementary. The attitudes, values, beliefs, and norms at Lakehills made me uncomfortable, and I recognized that nothing would change until I changed.

Systematic Experimentation

As I read, reflected, and discussed my "discoveries" in and through my coursework, it became evident that at the rate I was evolving, I might be nearing retirement before I realized the true nature of my feelings and professional goals. I requested and received a sabbatical leave—a year of intense reading, discussion, and reflection during which two problems became obvious. First, the teachers at Lakehills were content to remain isolated but congenial, and to avoid the responsibility of decisions in the isolated egg-crate classroom configuration that Dan Lortie (1975) described. The second problem was my benevolent authoritarian style of leadership. Under this leadership style, teachers preferred the isolated classroom structure. In order for teachers to become committed outside their classrooms, my style as a leader had to change.

I developed something like a plan of action: I named as a specific objective the creation of a council for shared decision making. I recognized that much of the plan would need to evolve as the situation unfolded, and so left the constitution, role, and procedures of the council undetermined.

SCHOOL CULTURE

School culture has been defined by Bower (1966) as the way professionals do things in schools; by Deal and Kennedy (1982) as shared beliefs and values that knit a community together; and by Schein (1985) as a pattern of basic assumptions that has worked well enough to be shared with new members as the correct way to do something. But Deal and Peterson (1990) best describe culture as follows:

> Each school has its own character or feel. You can sense it as you approach the building. You can almost smell and taste it as you walk through the doors . . . You can hear it in exchanges between students and teachers in the classroom and in students' talk with one another on the playground. (p. 7)

They go on to say,

> Culture is a powerful force. Trying to shape it, change it, or fight it can have serious repercussions. Principals who consciously try to influence or shape the culture of a school must be aware that there are pitfalls as well as positive outcomes. (p. 13)

Deal and Kennedy (1982) suggested that leaders should pay particular attention to shared beliefs, heroes and heroines, rituals, ceremonies, and stories—all elements of the symbolic or informal cultural network. When we reveal teachers' choices and we see the decisions they have made to make those choices, we can help them change their patterns, decisions, and school culture.

CRITICAL INCIDENTS IN THREE PERIODS OF CHANGE

As I moved through my study, reflection, and personal transformation, my changes necessarily influenced and affected the culture of Lakehills Elementary and the comfort of the people who worked there. Particularly as I initiated thoughtful action research, my own changes demanded deep change on the part of other school professionals: change in their behaviors, expectations, and relationships. This process of interdependent change can be seen through the following critical incidents during three distinct stages of change: business as usual, empowerment-initiated conflict, and truly shared governance.

Business as Usual: Top-Down Agenda Setting

Our first retreat was my first attempt to instill collegiality at Lakehills Elementary.

August 1992: The First Summer Retreat. I planned the agenda: to create a history of the school from 1958 to 1992, to perform some team-building activities, to discuss and create a school vision, and to have some time for the staff to socialize.

The retreat was held locally and teachers attended with some resistance. I noted in my journal that the staff was congenial and friendly but, as a group, avoided conflict and confrontation. At the time of the retreat and in later discussions with teachers I saw that the retreat was viewed as less than successful. I listed five reasons in my journal for that ineffectiveness of the retreat:

1. The 2-day retreat was cut to one day because of a hurricane. We attempted to compact a 2-day agenda into one day.
2. The planning for the retreat was done exclusively by the principal and the external facilitator. In addition, the facilitator was very task-oriented and seemed to be overly concerned with completing the agenda. A case in point happened during a discussion of the school history, when three different teachers mentioned inconsistency among teachers with regard to following through on rules. The facilitator passed over these comments because they did not seem to fit into the topic being discussed. At that point in the discussion, it appeared that about half of the staff stopped participating in the discussion.
3. The plan created by the facilitator and the principal called for the staff to create a core, shared vision—yet no prior discussion on mutually accepted values and principles on teaching had occurred. I noted in my journal after the retreat that process concerns such as basic group dynamics and essential core values (personal and professional) should have been discussed before a shared vision was attempted.

4. Regarding timing, teachers at our school usually used the 2 days prior to the school's opening for classroom preparation. I even observed some teachers cutting out bulletin board letters at the tables during the retreat.
5. Because this retreat was held in town, extended discussions and social interaction were minimal. Little opportunity was available for informal personal interaction.

August 1992: Canceled Group Presentations. During the planning of the first retreat, the facilitator and I assigned teacher groups to view a set of videotapes by John Goodlad that explained shared governance. The groups were asked to create a 5-minute presentation about the Goodlad information to start the retreat. The teachers were not happy with the prospect of meeting over the summer and planning the presentation, but agreed to perform the task. These presentations were then cut from the agenda when it was shortened due to the hurricane.

When the revised agenda was announced, the teachers expressed their disappointment through comments and facial expressions. Immediately after the retreat, the facilitator and I noted that this decision affected the entire retreat. In later focus group interviews conducted as part of my reflection and research, two different teachers mentioned that cutting the presentations without consulting the staff created an atmosphere of powerlessness from the start of the retreat.

Empowerment-Initiated Conflict

The leadership cabinet (formerly the principal's advisory group) consisted of a teacher elected from each grade level, one special education representative, and one staff member—each elected the previous year. The intent of the cabinet was to facilitate teacher input and communication among teachers.

September 1992: The Leadership Cabinet and Sabotage. I feared that, as in the past, some teachers would remain virtually silent as the topics were discussed in meetings, and then proceed to complain and sabotage the decision with others once they left the meeting. I decided to discuss the term "sabotage" during the first meeting and I suggested several verbal agreements about procedures. One agreement we reached was that no person would express negative opinions about the decisions of the cabinet unless he or she first expressed it to the group.

In focus group interviews, teachers identified a critical incident that occurred after this first meeting resulting in a new attitude and spirit of cooperation. The day following the first meeting, members of the leadership cabinet gave "informal" reports in the teachers' lounge. Two leadership cabinet members expressed negative feelings and opinions on topics about which they had been silent at the previous day's meeting. Another member of the leadership cabinet walked in during the discussion and remained in the lounge. At the beginning of the next leadership cabinet meeting, the teacher who had walked into the discussion brought up the sabotage.

The subsequent discussion was tense, loud, and uncomfortable. I remained silent—a very difficult task for me, and also unlike my previous style. The staff had taken control of policing itself even though conflict arose: I remained supportive of that, but silent. I felt the discussion ended with both sides achieving a higher degree of respect for one another and a better understanding of how sabotage can harm the staff.

September 1992: New Format for Faculty Meetings. Prior to 1992, faculty meetings had been held in the library, with everyone facing the same direction (usually at me). I would set the agenda, the majority of which concerned housekeeping tasks.

At our first faculty meeting of the 1992–1993 school year, we met instead in a teacher's classroom with the chairs in a circle. I wrote the housekeeping tasks in a bulletin distributed to teachers before the meeting. I sat in my chair for most of the meetings, except when using the chalkboard or overhead projector. I also adopted the habit of folding my arms as a reminder to myself to be silent as much as possible during all of the meetings. This caused one teacher to ask if my silence and folded arms were caused by anger. I recognized how others could misread this body language, but this interpretation was not mentioned again once I explained my aims.

The majority of the staff meetings were now centered on professional growth and teacher discussion. Healthy ways to engage in conflict were presented three different times, using three different methods, and each presentation was accompanied by constructive teacher discussions. I noted in my journal how hesitant the teachers were about confronting each other and about learning new methods for dealing with conflict. After each presentation, numerous teachers questioned why addressing conflict was important, argued that conflict didn't solve anything, and that learning assertive ways of approaching conflict was unnecessary.

October 1992: Rainy Day Decision. One teacher interviewed during the focus group interviews recalled the time a teacher who did not like to take risks or create conflict did both by making a decision that affected the entire staff.

A mist hung in the air, but some might not call that "rain." The teacher who came to me knew that the decision to call a rainy day schedule would be challenged by some of the other teachers. Rainy day schedules are very unpopular, because teachers do not get their time off during lunch.

The teacher came into my office and asked me whether we would move to a rainy day schedule. I remained noncommittal and asked the teacher what she thought. She said she would not make that decision. I told her I wasn't asking for her decision, but rather for her input.

She said that it was raining and too sloppy for the students to be on the yard. When I asked what she would do, she said she would impose a rainy day schedule. I saw progress in the teacher's willingness to make a commitment, if not a decision. I agreed with the teacher and made the change.

Another teacher observed during the focus group interviews, "Teachers are somewhat insecure . . . [they] do not like to make decisions that affect others."

November 1992: "I Don't Know". A major leap in trust occurred between the administration and teachers when the issue of a governing council was addressed at a faculty meeting in November. As the faculty rehashed discussions of teacher empowerment and site-based governance, the frustration I saw on the faces of the staff reflected my own growing disillusionment. The tiring discussion came to a head when one teacher asked me to explain just where we were going as a faculty.

Like others, she felt that I knew precisely where we were going; she wanted me to tell her how to get there—how the council was to look, how it was to work, and what part teachers played in the scheme of things. Teachers needed to get on about the business of doing their job, she felt. Deciding on the direction of the school was not part of that job.

The teachers and I fumbled around the discussion of the staff moving to a new uncertain destination, and other teachers, sensing that I did not have the answer, joined in to describe their discomfort. Finally, in utter frustration, I said that I did not know where we were going. I continued and stated that we would travel to our destination together, and the success of the journey rested as much on their shoulders as mine. As I looked up into the faces of the staff, their combined gaze of amazement and understanding excited as well as frightened me. In focus group interviews and in casual conversations, many teachers pointed to that meeting as a major turning point in the governing of Lakehills.

January 1993: Study Team in Houston. One of the most powerful collegial meetings occurred when half of the staff attended a National

Coalition for Equality in Learning (NCEL) Study Team in Houston near midyear. The success of this venture was predicated by half of the staff agreeing to go to Houston and paying most of their own expenses while the other half of the staff remained behind to expend much effort to keep the school going for 2 days.

The heated debate about the visit contained both superficial and deep issues. Some staff members wanted the growth. Four teachers who were near retirement supported the effort but did not see a need to attend the trip themselves. Others did not want the trip and attempted to sabotage the idea through overt as well as covert means. Overt sabotage primarily took place at the meeting where the trip was discussed, during which these teachers focused on the additional responsibilities—both financial and managerial—that the trip required. Covert sabotage occurred before and after the meeting, as these teachers tried to convince others not to attend. The example of one teacher in particular is logged in my journal.

A lower-grade teacher who loved teaching, participated in many professional growth activities, but was a friend of two of the saboteurs and avoided confrontation, became the target of the saboteurs. She wanted to attend, but was continually approached with various reasons not to: "Spending your own money is crazy," "Why should you do this on your time?" and "You won't learn anything new."

The teacher changed her mind almost daily, and came into my office and asked my opinion. I told her that I would support whatever decision she made. Just before the trip, she decided to go. Both during the trip and after, she told me how much she learned and enjoyed her newfound friendships.

In fact, the teachers attempting sabotage had little effect in the final analysis of this trip. I observed that, as the staff moved in a healthy collegial direction, sabotage became more difficult to achieve. Planning for the trip took on a life of its own as the staff learned to disagree, reach consensus, compromise, and afford due respect to all positions. In my year-end journal entry, I stated that this event constituted a major growth experience for the staff. As a good community of learners, half of the staff sacrificed for the growth of the other half.

February 1993: Teacher Selection for the Governance Council. About midyear I recorded in my journal how conflict was valued and embraced more fully by teachers. Simultaneously, discussions on the creation of the site Governance Council became heated. In the final construction of the council, there were to be seven teachers, seven parents (including two Parent Teacher Organization officers), two community members, a staff representative, and the principal. Three town meetings, which involved all stakeholders, were held to decide the criteria for all aspects of the council. The decision about the number and distribution of council members was made at town meetings, but the decision of how the teaching positions would be distributed was left to the teachers.

In a staff meeting, teachers decided to distribute the positions among upper and lower grades, with one at large. Then one teacher asked what would happen if all of the elected teachers were white or black. The teachers decided to elect four of the teachers on an initial ballot (two upper- and two lower-grade teachers), then elect the remaining three to insure healthy racial representation. The entire staff shared a palpable feeling of accomplishment upon reaching this decision.

When the voting actually occurred, all but three teachers removed their names from the second ballot, and four black and three white teachers represented the staff at governance council. The assurance of equal representation was accomplished, but more importantly, the volatile topic of race relations was introduced, discussed, and settled. A negotiated settlement left teachers feeling good about how the council was to be composed and about their ability to manage conflict.

Phase Three, Shared Governance

I had roughed out a plan for the second retreat, which the leadership cabinet could refine and adapt to suit staff needs. My plan was to develop grade-level visions that could be combined into a school-level vision.

March 1993: Setting the Agenda. During a leadership cabinet meeting, this plan was placed on an overhead projector and changes were recorded as they were suggested. Soon, the transparency became difficult to read. The committee kept coming back to the idea that some underlying issues had not been resolved and would prevent the staff from reaching any consensus. After nearly an hour of heated discussion, I quietly removed the transparency from the overhead projector and replaced it with a new, blank sheet. The staff noticed the change and watched me for some indication of my feelings. A smile and a quick, "OK, now let's plan our retreat," made the teachers aware of my support.

The facilitator in attendance at the meeting later commented, "The biggest change I've seen was the meeting with your core group where we planned the second retreat. Remember how you had it all laid out and about halfway through the meeting you tore the paper up and started over? I felt a trust build that is hard to describe. It's as if the teachers there said, 'He really means this is our show.'"

April 1993: The Teacher Strike Discussion. Planning for the second retreat was a friendly and, at times, even humorous, struggle between the teachers on the leadership cabinet and me, still evolving as a leader and principal. Specifically, they wanted to talk about hostilities left over from a teachers' strike 3 years earlier. My journal records my repeated resistance to discuss the 3-year-old strike, as well as the teachers' persistence—which resulted in a retreat agenda that reflected their concerns.

At the retreat, the strike discussion began with strikers and nonstrikers meeting in separate groups, answering questions about their position and the other side's position. Each side then presented to the group as a whole. Special rules on questions and clarifications were instituted by the facilitators to help reduce hostility and open confrontation. The separate groups met for over an hour. The presentations, with discussions and questions, lasted over 2 hours.

Each group met again, creating a representation of what they learned about themselves and the other side from the exercise. These presentations and the subsequent discussion stretched long into the night. Tempers flared and tears flowed, but through it all, teachers seemed to want to resolve this and move on. For all of us, it seemed time to move on.

The discussion centered around personal beliefs, personalities, and acceptance of the opinions of others. The inappropriate behavior of two teachers during the strike (both had moved on to other schools) was also a sticky subject that was addressed and resolved. The heart of the discussion was about hurt feelings, a competitive attitude promoted by the school district administration for teachers who remained on campus during the strike, and a similar attitude promoted by the teachers' union. The retreat rebuilt trust, healed relationships, and allowed staff to begin to work together again. While the rebuilt trust was cautiously given, the repair began.

Because of the trust the facilitators felt already existed among the staff, they allowed the discussion to continue until midnight—long past the 6:00 p.m. scheduled stopping time. The facilitators concluded that the staff had underestimated the amount of trust they already shared, and needed this extended time to discover it for and among themselves.

May 1993: Sixth Grade Departmentalization. Near the end of the school year, the sixth grade teachers came to me to ask about departmental teaching. The 3 sixth grade teachers had come to me with the same idea about 3 years earlier and knew that I believed that the self-contained elementary classroom was the most productive approach to school organization.

I pointed out that some logistical arrangements would have to be made—not the least of which was gaining the agreement of the next year's parents and the sixth grade resource teacher. The teachers met over the next 3 weeks to develop schedules and iron out the anticipated problems of the endeavor. When we met again, they explained that problems such as schedules, textbooks, subject time requirements, and the like had been eliminated. I was informed that a loose survey of parents yielded mixed, but mostly positive, reviews. The teachers had just a few items remaining to be worked out with my help.

I recognized that it took collegiality (heated discussion arriving at a shared solution) to reach the level of agreement the teachers had achieved. The teachers had engaged in some level of risk-taking when they approached me once again with a suggestion they knew I did not initially support. Although only four teachers were facing me, at the time I felt I faced many more teachers, parents, and staff members—all those who waited to see if I would give up control and go against my initial feeling to support these four teachers. The decision to move forward with a departmental structure was critical in staff—and personal—growth.

May 1993: Continuation of the Arts Program. During the end-of-the-year staff meeting, we discussed the continuation of the school's arts program. After I explained the district staffing formula (how teachers are allocated to schools), two opposing sides immediately came to the forefront. One group of teachers was willing to take an extra student or two in their classrooms in order to free up one and a half teaching positions for art and music teachers. The other group sought to eliminate the arts program and so achieve reduced class sizes for all remaining teachers.

Those who sought to cut the arts program were the most vocal, and dominated the conversation for at least the first 10 minutes. Then a teacher spoke up about how all children need the arts, and how some learn better when the arts are incorporated in their studies. In a fiery comeback, the opposing side used personal power as well as volume to squelch the dissent. The arts eliminators folded their arms and crossed their legs when not talking. They waved their arms, and one even stood up—a rare occurrence—when they took the floor. They seemed to direct their comments to the less vocal and perhaps more timid staff members.

One voice, a kindergarten teacher, spoke of the need for the arts program. This courage seemed to inspire the other staff members and they began to support her position to keep the arts. Another voice and then another spoke up, until it was clear that the arts program would stay. An overwhelming number of teachers supported the proposal.

REFLECTION

In 1997, Shirley Hord published a monograph, *Professional Learning Communities: Communities of Continuous Inquiry and Improvement*, that brought me new understanding of the change process I had begun and experienced. Hord's synthesis of research on schools as learning organizations provided a new framework for my findings. The elements I had identified as critical to Lakehills' change process were vision, conflict, professional development, trust, time, and leadership through empowerment and communication. Hord characterized communities of continuous inquiry and improvement as including collective inquiry, shared leadership, shared vision, shared personal practice, and supportive conditions (both physical and people-related). This study and Hord's work reveal that most of the characteristics are common in both works. Examples of this congruence are Hord's shared vision and vision in this study, shared leadership (Hord) and empowerment (study), collective inquiry (Hord) and professional development (study), shared personal practice (Hord) paired with trust and conflict (study).

The incidents shared in this chapter demonstrate an evolution over time—an evolution of a staff, an evolution of a principal, and perhaps the evolution of a school into a learning community.

At Lakehills, much of the power and authority initially resided in the principal's hands—as demonstrated by staff meetings where everyone faced the principal, or retreats planned exclusively by the principal and outside facilitator. Then the teachers asked, "Where are we going?" and heard the principal respond, "I don't know." This answer made some uncomfortable and led others to understand the fluid nature of change.

Conflict, which was avoided at all cost at the beginning of the study, became progressively more open and accepted. First, sabotage was confronted, and then, through time, the staff moved to a level of confidence that allowed them to give voice to their desires, even when these desires were in direct conflict with the preferences of the principal. Perhaps more significantly, they gained the confidence to disagree with one another deeply and loudly, and to come to decisions nevertheless. The benefits of shared personal practice, the responsibilities of shared leadership, and the potential of a shared and articulated vision outweighed their discomfort with conflict.

The value attached to professional growth also evolved. Mistrust and avoidance of professional growth had been widely accepted, and was demonstrated in the cautious attendance at the first in-town retreat. Professional development had been seen as top-down directives, focused on personal deficits. But by midyear, the entire school collaborated in supporting half the staff's attendance at a study team in Houston. At year's end, full participation in the planning and engaged attendance at the out-of-town spring retreat demonstrated the new value teachers placed on the opportunity to come together in "collective inquiry," to learn more about teaching—and one another.

Finally, the school experienced and benefited from an evolution in governance. Fragmented governance had been in place: teachers were represented by an appointed advisory committee, parents by a PTO board, and community members only on an as-needed basis. These groups were narrowly focused, usually in place for a 1-year term, and often worked at cross-purposes. These groups were primarily advisory in nature—the principal retained power and control.

Now, a school governance council, composed of representatives of all the stakeholders and focused on long-range concerns, has the power to address any concern. The principal's voice is one among many on the governance council, and leadership is shared among the stakeholders. As a result, the school is vital, energetic, and still the premier elementary school in the district. Its principalship—although transformed—remains a coveted leadership position.

IMPLICATIONS FOR PRACTICE

Two years after beginning the governance council at Lakehills Elementary, I was transferred to a troubled junior high school. Worchester Junior High School had little similarity to Lakehills: Worchester was much larger, with nearly 1,200 students; it experienced difficulty in succeeding almost from its beginning; student test scores were below average; the 15.5-acre facility was in disrepair; teachers felt isolated and unsupported; and student discipline was a major issue. The lessons I learned at Lakehills became the cornerstone of my administrative life at Worchester, as I set out to create a learning community marked by collegiality and shared leadership, trust, and an acceptance of the natural conflicts that arise when teaching professionals care deeply about their work, their students, and their school.

At Lakehills, I had learned the value of listening first before changes were proposed. I applied this new belief at Worchester by holding a brunch about a month before school began. There, I simply listened as the staff told me their three greatest strengths and three greatest struggles. This meeting led us to create four acting committees to address the issues of student discipline, student attendance, textbooks, and curriculum. These committees met before school started in order to plan ways to improve their focus areas. By the first day of school, these plans had been created and garnered substantial teacher support. My only act had been allowing teachers to solve the problems they had identified.

Disagreements arose at this first brunch meeting and throughout the year. I worked with the staff to improve confrontation and negotiation skills, thus helping to create an atmosphere in which teachers were responsible for themselves and their school. As a result, teachers felt an increased sense of power over their own lives and their environment.

My experience at Lakehills taught me that shared leadership is not always welcomed. I began my tenure at Worchester with the expectation that the teachers would be leaders. Frankly, many of the staff preferred that I lead and they follow, but complained. Learning from my experience at Lakehills, I created conditions to support this shared leadership by forming two teacher teams at each grade level, reassigning rooms so that team members' rooms were adjacent. I requested that each team of 5 to 6 teachers meet twice each month to discuss student and curriculum issues. These teams began working together to solve problems and support one another—the beginnings of shared practice within a collegial environment.

Each teacher team then selected one member to serve on the Core Team. The Core Team functioned as the major body of the school. All new ideas were either generated from or presented to the Core Team, whose members then returned to their teacher teams to elicit comments from throughout the professional staff. My challenge was to hear problems and concerns, and to allow individuals and teachers to refine solutions and procedures. My willingness to allow teachers to lead promoted teacher risk-taking, increased their openness, and allowed us all to address school-related issues.

Through the course of this study and the beginnings of my tenure as principal at Worchester, I have discovered a few apparent paradoxes, which I feel are essential to successful leadership:

- Sharing power increases power. The strength of an administrator is the power and authority that workers choose to give their leader. The power given to a principal by the central office is short-lived if it is not utilized to create shared leadership and shared responsibility among all the stakeholders in a school community.
- Disorder begs increased control; but leadership, not control, is the cure.
- Do the right thing even when it feels impractical, impossible, or hurts your heart.
- Shared leadership is more difficult to create and maintain. It is

    messy, time consuming, frustrating, and will anger some of the staff—do it anyway.

- A dogma of independence and interdependence at the same time is difficult and necessary in creating a collaborative school culture.

As school leaders, what we are asked to do in building a learning community is analogous to what we ask teachers to achieve with a class of students, that is, help them to come together to learn and grow in the hope that one day they can themselves lead.

CHAPTER 11

Against All Odds:
Reculturing a Troubled School

Dianne F. Olivier

Sergiovanni (1994) proposed that a school be viewed as a community with shared ideas, in which bonding between people and control is exercised through norms, purposes, values, professional socialization, collegiality, and natural interdependence. Implicit within this notion of community is the factor of culture. When focusing on school culture to foster school improvement, it is necessary to recognize the interpersonal interactions and social processes that shape that culture (Cavanagh & Dellar, 1997). The values and norms of individuals are transformed into the collective values and norms constituting the culture. Because of this, changing school cultures can be very challenging—it entails altering long-held beliefs, expectations, and habits. Hargreaves (1995) noted that developing collaborative cultures entails *reculturing* the school from a focus on individual teachers or balkanized teacher subgroups. This chapter provides a narrative of reculturing, undertaken by one principal at a troubled elementary school.

When she arrived at Live Oaks Elementary in 1997, Principal Debbie Bergeron entered a school facing multiple crises, including high staff turnover and low student achievement. She quickly came to recognize that these crises resulted from a school culture that allowed teachers to believe they were not ultimately responsible for the learning their students accomplished—or failed to accomplish. Out of this failure to connect teaching and learning issued a number of negative behaviors and beliefs: Live Oaks Elementary faced high rates of teacher transfers and administrative turnover; teachers and students maintained high absentee numbers; disciplinary problems caused disruptions in teaching and sapped administrative energy; teachers worked in isolation and expressed low expectations of students; students failed in high numbers; and the community as a whole had little trust in Live Oaks Elementary. In the 10 years before Debbie Bergeron took over the principalship, six individuals had entered and left that post at Live Oaks. Many of her predecessors had experienced little success in improving the school, perhaps because they failed to focus on school culture.

YEAR 1: FIGHTING THE STATUS QUO

In this first year, the challenges were formidable, the first of which was teachers' expectations of students' performance.

Challenging Expectations

Live Oaks Elementary, comprised of grades 4–6, has a population of approximately 600 students of which 66% are African American, 33% Caucasian, and 1% Asian and Hispanic. A majority (82.3%) of Live Oaks' students are economically disadvantaged. The staff includes 32 professional teachers, a curriculum coordinator, a behavior interventionist, and a reading facilitator. The year Debbie became principal, several teachers had retired, resigned, or transferred out of the school (some voluntarily, others not). Although her predecessor had filled a few positions, Debbie faced the task of interviewing and recommending the appointment of eight new staff members. Live Oaks was Debbie's first administrative position; thus, the experience of selecting teachers was quite new. Her intent, however, was clear: to select knowledgeable, energetic teachers who would infuse new blood into a stagnant faculty.

After addressing these staffing concerns, Debbie looked to student performance, developing a plan to remediate the many academic shortcomings. In this effort she had to contend with incomplete and minimal records regarding achievement data, financial status, and school and district policies and procedures—her "inheritance" from the previous principal who had been released of his duties due to poor performance. Through classroom observations of teachers' performance and review of their lesson plans, Debbie immediately noted significant problems. There was an alarming lack of consistency in teacher planning, preparation, and presentation of the required academic curriculum.

Prior to becoming principal at Live Oaks, Debbie had been recognized as an outstanding elementary school teacher and as a specialist in the state teacher assessment program. As a new principal, she relied on the strengths she had developed as a teacher, and spent many hours in classroom observation. These observations included assessing the components of effective teaching. Debbie had hoped that her in-depth observations would serve as a positive influence in promoting teaching and learning, but instead, she met with extreme resistance from most teachers.

Many Live Oaks teachers accepted and expected low student achievement, and did not connect low performance with a need to improve their instruction. Historically, Live Oaks' principals had reinforced this denial of responsibility by spending minimal time observing the teaching and learning process within the classrooms, predictably and consistently awarding teachers with ratings of "satisfactory"—the highest possible rating on the state evaluations.

In contrast, Debbie's classroom observations reflected specific lesson areas and teaching methods that she deemed in need of improvement. She documented those areas, and rated some teachers' performance as "unsatisfactory." Many teachers expressed outrage that the new principal would question their methods and strategies, actually document the need for improvement, and reflect their unsatisfactory performance on evaluations.

Building Trust

While Debbie's evaluations were unpopular, they clearly communicated the need for teacher improvement and school change. Through her day-to-day interactions with faculty and observations of interactions between various faculty members, Debbie began to realize that a lack of trust among teachers and between teachers and administration was preventing the school from change. Discussions of ongoing school procedures or presentation of new ideas by the principal usually resulted in virtually little or no staff dialogue, openly negative attitudes from some teachers, skepticism from others, and little cooperation among faculty members.

Live Oaks Elementary operated with a minimal administrative staff. In addition to the principal, teacher leaders assumed the roles of curriculum coordinator and reading facilitator. After carefully assessing the operations within the school, Debbie and this support staff realized they needed to create opportunities that would reduce teacher isolation by fostering the teachers' experience of working as a team. Although the initial attempts resulted in limited participation, the opportunities for collaborative work by grade level and content level began slowly to have an impact on the staff. The teachers began to buy in to the notion that together they could change Live Oaks Elementary.

Debbie and her immediate support staff were open to suggestions and received continued support and assistance from the superintendent and central office staff. When Debbie discovered that the school leadership team existed on paper only, she restructured it to reflect representation from all grade levels and all programs within the school. She and the school's new leadership team held sessions that stressed administrative and teacher leadership, school improvement planning, and development of a focus on student performance—especially the performance of those students deemed to be most at risk of failure.

While several teachers began to accept the challenge to improve the school's academic status, a small group of teachers thwarted any and all attempts at progress. This group formed a vocal minority that managed to diffuse many attempts to move forward. They believed the low performance of students was preordained by student socioeconomic status and lack of parental involvement. They resented a principal who pushed for change, who suggested that instruction might indeed play a critical role in student academic success or failure.

Then everything changed. Kelly, one of the bright new young teachers at Live Oaks, was killed in an automobile accident while returning home from school on a clear November afternoon. The faculty and the principal were profoundly affected by the loss of this energetic and enthusiastic teacher. The rancor that had risen among some teachers, or between teachers and the administration, softened in the aftermath of Kelly's death.

Kelly had stepped forward at the onset of the school year and assisted in moving the school in a positive direction. She was actively involved in trying to make a difference among her colleagues. Specifically, Kelly was involved in the school's effort to achieve reform through the use of research-based efforts. The faculty recognized her efforts and realized the need to proceed. This tragic event contributed to the initial development of teacher leaders and helped establish a norm of sharing ideas through the study of research.

The year concluded with the faculty voting its approval for the implementation of a school-wide reading program, Success for All (SFA), designed to target the needs of all students within the school. SFA had been implemented at Live Oaks' feeder school, and primary-level teachers reported their progress in raising student achievement through the program. For implementation at Live Oaks, it was essential that the majority of the faculty express a willingness to adopt the program. The final faculty vote indicated an 80% acceptance rate. The principal, teachers, and central office staff considered this faculty endorsement and their commitment to implement the SFA program to be a significant step forward in whole-school improvement.

YEAR 2: SPEED BUMPS ON THE PATH OF TRANSITION

Although her entire first year seemed to present a struggle for Debbie, she was enthusiastic to begin year two. Test scores were still significantly below state and district averages, but the extensive training being provided to teachers in reading raised hopes for improving the students' low reading levels. During the summer before Debbie's second year, it became quite clear that she would begin the school year with many new teachers. Some teachers who were resistant to change elected to move to other positions outside of Live Oaks or to enter retirement. Fifteen new faculty members were hired to replace teachers who retired or transferred. Debbie saw this as an opportunity to bring on new teachers who were willing to assume those challenges facing the teachers and students.

Transition through Research

The implementation of the research-based SFA reading program allowed teachers to address the students on their specific grade level. Thus, if a fourth grade student's reading level was above or below grade four, his or her instruction was delivered at his or her appropriate level. A new school norm developed: the 90-minute reading block became sacred. There were no interruptions from outside or within the school, and all teachers and students were actively involved in a structured reading program. Results surfaced immediately. Although the faculty were aware that significant improvement school-wide would take time (research indicates a 5-year span is the norm for institutionalized change), there were specific instances of student progress. Accompanying the concentrated reading program was a slight decrease in disciplinary referrals. Attendance rates among teachers began to improve and a new emphasis was placed on student attendance. Failure rates of students began to decline.

However, Debbie noticed that both the reading program and the behavior/disciplinary program, Boys Town, were not being implemented in a consistent manner school-wide. Since both SFA and Boys Town are research-based models, the faculty was aware of the necessity to follow program specifics to achieve the intended results. The lack of consistency in SFA implementation surfaced during the fall implementation visit by the Success for All consultants. These consultants spent time in each teacher's class and noted that approximately half of the teachers were not implementing the program according to the model, thus jeopardizing the potential for school-wide improvement.

Debbie called upon central office staff to assist in the school's internal monitoring of the reading program. With a concerted effort from the supervisory staff, more effective monitoring by the principal and reading facilitator, additional in-house support, and informal and formal in-service sessions for teachers, the follow-up spring implementation visit indicated improvement in the SFA implementation.

Another issue facing Live Oaks was the need to deal with several students who had severe emotional problems. A Reflection Center was established within the school to address these students' disciplinary problems through in-school interventions that offered more individualized attention and services.

PLC Initiation

Debbie was offered and accepted a significant opportunity for Live Oaks to participate in a project aimed at developing a professional learning community. This opportunity through SEDL would support current efforts in school-wide improvement by providing technical support, strategies, and structures for measuring and guiding school reform. In particular, Debbie and her support staff hoped that involvement in the Creating Communities of Continuous Inquiry and Improvement initiative would promote shared leadership skills at Live Oaks.

In the fall of 1998, the faculty completed the survey *School Professional Staff as Learning Community* (Hord, 1996). This measure assessed the perceptions of the school staff as a learning organization in terms of democratic participation, shared vision, collective learning, supportive conditions, shared instructional practices, and improvement strategies. The instrument provided Live Oaks an opportunity to take a "baseline" reading of the effects of previous initiatives—the newly structured leadership teams' real implementation of shared leadership, for instance, and the impact of Success for All on collective learning among faculty.

The results of the PLC survey indicated that the school rated itself high on the component of collective learning. However, when the school leadership committee discussed these findings, there was a consensus that collective learning existed primarily due to district and state mandates or in the implementation of programs like SFA. The leadership team was still concerned about the minimal amount of voluntary collective learning among staff members and the continued resistance to rigorous collegial observation and evaluation of instruction. Live Oaks faculty had yet to reach the desired level of trust that would support collective assessment of their work and suggestions for more collegial learning and interaction about learning.

The 1998–1999 school year drew to a close with indications of continued improvement, although some issues of concern remained unresolved. After approval of the new school-wide reading program, reading component meetings fostered more collegial work among teachers, teachers initiated planning sessions for lesson preparation, inter-classroom visits were conducted, and lesson components were modeled among teachers.

But a high level of distrust still existed among certain faculty members, and continued resistance to change was evidenced by a tendency for faculty to resort to old teaching methods behind closed doors.

At the close of the year, the school received a School Performance Score (SPS) of 43.7. This score was based upon the new State Accountability Program and characterized Live Oaks Elementary as "academically below average." The SPS was comprised of student performance on the Grade 4 LEAP 21 (a criterion-referenced test in Language Arts and mathematics based on newly adopted content standards), the Grades 5 and 6 Iowa Test of Basic Skills, norm-referenced tests, and student attendance rates. Teachers were disappointed at the school's designation after a year of hard work and some improvement. But they were also realistic in acknowledging that progress could be made in meeting the academic needs of Live Oaks students.

Due to the SPS, Live Oaks was eligible to receive a grant through the Comprehensive School Reform Demonstration (CSRD) program. A proposal including resources for school-wide improvement in reading was submitted and funded for implementation the following school year. At the conclusion of the 1998–1999 school session, Live Oaks' school-wide plan was assessed through the School Support Team Review process. The School Support Team, composed of the district reading supervisor, external educators outside of the school, and a principal from within the district, evaluated the current school-wide plan and assisted the school in developing goals and objectives for the upcoming school year. These goals were: (1) to improve academic performance in reading and math; (2) to develop a school-wide discipline plan; and (3) to increase parental involvement.

YEAR 3: TRANSITION TO TRANSFORMATION

The 1999–2000 school year for Live Oaks Elementary began smoothly, with an increasingly experienced and trusted principal still at the helm. However, another large teacher turnover created the need for training to prepare new staff to implement the strategies and methods recently adopted at Live Oaks. Numerous professional development sessions provided new teachers with necessary training in the areas of the reading components, learning styles, math concepts, crisis intervention, and disciplinary strategies. Also, the sessions prepared new teachers to enter a school culture that increasingly valued and insisted upon continued and collective learning.

Two teachers who had experienced a "True Colors" session at a National Aeronautics and Space Administration-sponsored science workshop brought that staff development session back to Live Oaks. With the support of the principal, the pair led their colleagues through a session designed to provide opportunities for teachers to investigate their learning styles and formulate plans to foster collaborative work. Teachers were asked to complete the Myers Briggs Type Indicator, which helps identify a person's specific temperament. Through this assessment, each staff member earned an individual color designation, which proved revealing on a personal, as well as group, level. The activity was intended to build understanding and rapport between faculty and staff members by identifying individual personality types and leadership style preferences. In essence, faculty members were trying to determine what made their colleagues tick, as well as what ticked them off. By experimenting and learning why people react and interact in a certain manner, faculty members began to understand the necessity of considering personality temperament in working collaboratively as a team. "True Colors," which allowed Live Oaks teachers to experience learning together through the leadership of colleagues, served as a critical incident for the staff upon which additional success could be built.

Additional professional development provided continued opportunities for collective learning, focused on lingering issues of concern. Crisis Prevention Intervention helped teachers address severe disciplinary disruptions through nonviolent methods of intervention in potentially explosive situations. These strategies enhanced teacher skills for de-escalating situations involving disruptive students before the incidents got out of hand. Teachers gained confidence in dealing with disruptive students and felt secure in keeping students and teachers in a safe environment.

Another key program introduced into Live Oaks Elementary was "In Touch with Parents." This program was designed to strengthen the level and depth of active parent participation by developing teacher-parent collaboration to enhance student learning. The school made a concerted effort to get in touch with parents and sponsor activities to spark parental interest. A "Second Cup of Coffee" was instituted at school as a way to integrate the parents into the school in a nonthreatening manner. This informal morning gathering fostered interactions between parents and individuals involved in their children's education. Parents were invited to have a cup of coffee and conversation with several key individuals including the school superintendent, a juvenile judge, school psychologists, and high-profile community members. These opportunities allowed parents to set the agenda, focus on issues of their choice, ask as few or as many questions as they wished, and to talk with key decision makers. Parents were encouraged to suggest topics for conversations and to indicate who was to be invited into the conversations. The school also increased daytime opportunities for interacting with parents in a proactive manner.

In support of the school's goal to improve student performance in mathematics, teachers were offered training during the summer months and throughout the school year in math strategies targeting identified weaknesses. In keeping with PLC values, much of this ongoing professional development was provided in a collegial and classroom-based manner: a district-level mathematics lead teacher spent one day per week with teachers at Live Oaks. This math facilitator served in a nonevaluative manner and extended math assistance through numerous opportunities. Her services included meeting with teachers by grade level and math content area and demonstrating math techniques that could be utilized within the classroom. The reception to the math lead teacher was mixed: several teachers objected to the necessary changes in teaching the content standards and relearning mathematics concepts, but others appreciated the assistance in math.

As a CSRD grant recipient, Live Oaks Elementary was invited to participate in a State School Improvement Conference. A diverse group— including the principal, teachers from each grade level, special services personnel, support staff, a parent representative, a school board member, and two central office staff members—represented Live Oaks Elementary. The conference featured national speakers and small-group sessions designed to allow the school team to work collaboratively in planning for the new school session.

Live Oaks team members returned to the school and enthusiastically shared information with the entire faculty. Ideas and new strategies were generated that targeted increased teacher and student involvement in the pursuit of academic improvement. Teachers suggested several strategies to assist the students, including extended day academic tutorial programs, think time for disciplinary problems, in-school suspension, parent calls and contacts, steps for more effective monitoring of students' behavioral and academic performance, and checks for effective implementation of the reading program.

At a school-wide staff development session, two teachers made a presentation to the faculty on the school's involvement and progress toward professional learning community activities. While the model of the PLC had not been overtly highlighted as the model of school improvement for the school, the principal and support staff had been incorporating activities and methods designed to move the school toward a more unified vision, having teachers actively involved in leadership roles, providing opportunities for collective learning and application of this learning, addressing school structures (such as time and scheduling issues) and personnel that would support these changes, and spending time formally and informally sharing teaching practices.

The teacher presentation highlighting the way Live Oaks operated as a PLC was extremely positive and well received. The staff had accepted the need to embrace change. Although a few teachers lagged behind, the majority of the teachers were beginning to display an attitude of "whatever it takes" to improve achievement. Their renewed interest and excitement in working toward school success seemed to permeate the faculty.

Comprehensive School Assessment

As a result of its low SPS, Live Oaks Elementary was invited to participate in a new aspect of the State Accountability model. The school chose to participate in the District Assistance Team (DAT) model. This thorough evaluation of the school status involved a team of five central office staff members. The process included comprehensive classroom observations of all teachers based on components of effective teaching and effective classroom strategies; questionnaires for the principal, teachers, parents, and students; one-on-one teacher interviews with one third of the faculty; a principal interview; teacher focus groups with one third of the faculty; and student focus groups. All questionnaires, interviews, and focus groups were designed to assess perceptions regarding satisfaction with overall school performance including academic norms, academic efficacy, safe and orderly environment, expectations, leadership, quality of instruction, parent-school relationships, and professional development. The results produced pertinent information that was valuable in planning and working toward school-wide improvement.

The teachers expressed dissatisfaction with being labeled a low-performing school and stressed their interest in improving student performance. The one-on-one teacher interviews revealed displeasure with those teachers who attempted to diffuse all strategies that were targeted toward change for the purpose of improvement. Most faculty members did not like the negative perception the community had of them, and wanted to actively change these perceptions. The individual teacher interviews and teacher focus groups expressed a need for leadership stability at the administrative and teacher level. Faculty believed that the high turnover rates adversely affected the school's performance.

While the parent surveys expressed high expectations for their children and the general agreement that the school was not adequately meeting their needs, the teacher surveys still appeared to limit the capabilities of the students, thus providing evidence of low expectations from the teachers. The students very candidly expressed their opinions, ranging from displeasure of the school uniforms (district policy) to concern when certain teachers did not "actively" teach. The students indicated a desire for all teachers to hold all students accountable and the need for all teachers to take responsibility for the learning process among the students. The DAT process afforded the teachers at Live Oaks an opportunity to view their school performance through multiple perspectives.

Reaching for Results

As the tremendous amount of work continued at all levels of the school, the spring testing period came around quickly. Teachers and students were quite apprehensive. Although many activities addressing required content standards had been implemented, there was a feeling that a little more time would be beneficial. The teachers at Live Oaks believed they had rallied to the challenge. Their school had instituted the most comprehensive tutoring program throughout the district with 16 teachers involved in the after-school tutorial program. But was this enough?

Prior to receiving the results regarding student performance, the Live Oaks faculty took an unexpected step. While reading performance was improving through SFA, the faculty was requested to vote on the continuation of the program. Much to the surprise of the principal, the 80% faculty approval rate was not sustained. While 60% of the teachers wanted to continue the reading program, 40% expressed dissatisfaction and wanted to dispense with the program.

Debbie and her teacher support staff were disappointed and disheartened by the vote. Why would teachers discard a program in which students were succeeding? The superintendent met with the Live Oaks teacher leadership team and inquired as to the reasons for the disapproval. While few teachers openly expressed their feelings, some mentioned the stringent requirements and the extensive teacher preparation that was necessary to implement the program according to guidelines. The superintendent requested that the leadership team think seriously about the consequences of abandoning the program. He also challenged the team to discuss alternatives that could take the place of SFA. However, in an important gesture that underscored the administration's commitment to real shared leadership, the superintendent expressed his willingness to go along with the teachers' decision, even if he disagreed with it.

End-of-the year results indeed indicated improvement! Seventy percent of fourth grade students passed the Language Arts test, an increase of 5% over the previous year; and 64% of the students were successful on the mathematics test, a dramatic 30-point increase over the previous year's 34% success rate. With the incorporation of the DEEP Into Mathematics Program that retrained teachers in math concepts and the additional time-on-task that was spent in the extended-day math activities, the teachers did indeed observe significant improvement in the academic performance of the students. The increase in student performance, combined with improved student attendance, contributed to an increase in the SPS from the original 43.7 to 55.8. While this score still categorized the school as performing "academically below average," the increase demonstrated attainment of Live Oaks' 2-year growth target. The only elementary school in the district to reach its 2-year growth target, Live Oaks had made significant strides indeed.

Shortly after Live Oaks received the state performance results, the faculty had an open discussion regarding the success of their students. The staff acknowledged that their students had performed at a much higher level, the reading performance and reading levels of the students were improving, the rate of failure had decreased, and there was definitely evidence that Success for All—regardless of the amount of preparation—was beneficial to their students. Thus, the school staff decided to continue implementing SFA. Another meeting was requested with the superintendent and he was apprized of the school's decision. While teachers at Live Oaks encountered a bump in the road to their progress, clear indications of success led them to adjust, maneuver past the incident, and continue on the pathway to success.

CONCLUSION

Student performance on the state tests excited both teachers and students at Live Oaks. The staff felt they had made major steps toward adapting to change and toward addressing the needs of their students through the Schoolwide Improvement Plan. With academic movement in a positive direction, Live Oaks was beginning to observe the ripple effects that occur when students and teachers are challenged and improve their performance. An end-of-the year report on disciplinary referrals indicated a 55% decrease in behavior referrals, a 44% decrease in out-of-school suspensions, a 60% reduction for in-school suspensions, and a decrease of 65% in Saturday detentions over the previous year. The school staff concurred that the implementation of several programs, behavioral and academic, contributed to the improved school setting.

The culture of Live Oaks no longer included low expectations for students, staff, or parents. Students were being challenged in academic and behavioral terms, parents were becoming more involved, and the awareness of academic and behavioral expectations had increased. All of the efforts by the school staff had contributed to improved performance by students and teachers.

As the third year of Debbie's leadership of Live Oaks came to a close, the school established plans for remediation for those students who had been unsuccessful on the state tests. A large percentage of the teachers at Live Oaks applied to teach in the summer remedial program, thus indicating their renewed commitment to the students and community of Live Oaks Elementary.

A key factor in the change process at any school is the need to address significant areas or issues in a manner that will result in sustainability. Cuban (1990) has categorized educational reform as either first- or second-order changes. First-order changes, or surface-level changes, are those that improve the efficiency and effectiveness of what is currently done without affecting the basic organizational features. These can be seen in changes such as adjustments in the school schedule or in planning time for teachers, changes in duty rosters, extended school hours, or new school uniforms. Second-order changes, the more critical of the two, strive to alter the fundamental ways in which organizations are put together, including new goals, structures, and roles. These changes tend to be focused on addressing the beliefs, values, assumptions, and norms within the school. The challenge of the 1990s has been to focus on more second-order changes in order to affect the culture and structure of schools (Fullan & Stiegelbauer, 1991).

Live Oaks Elementary has not only begun addressing those first-order changes that improve the efficiency and effectiveness of the current program; they have begun to give attention to the more difficult second-order changes by altering the fundamental operations and norms of the school. The restructuring and reculturing of Live Oaks is including more interactive participation between the teachers and the principal and among the teachers, increased teacher decision-making, emphasis on teacher leaders and sharing of leadership responsibilities, increased teacher collaboration, and sharing of personal practice. The faculty has recently begun to celebrate the successes that occur at Live Oaks Elementary and to share with the community the changes that are taking place. At district meetings, they are no longer content to sit in the back and listen to the accomplishments of other elementary schools within the district—now Live Oaks faculty want to announce their own accomplishments in school improvement.

Debbie and the Leadership Council recognize that although Live Oaks has made significant strides, the changes that are being implemented are not yet internalized. Working as a team, they will continue to lead their school forward toward significant improvement in the teaching and learning process regardless of the odds.

CHAPTER 12

The Superintendent's Influence on the Creation of a Professional Learning Community: A Story of School Transition

Anita Pankake

Many forces, some positive, some negative, impinge on any school district committed to transforming the existing organization to one that is an authentic professional learning community. According to Fullan and Stiegelbauer (1991), "The district administrator is the single most important individual for setting the expectation and tone of the pattern of change within the local district" (p. 191). This chapter examines the way in which changes at the district level influenced the interpersonal and professional relationships at a high school that was trying to become a professional learning community. It describes the ways in which school professionals can become distracted from a focus on campus-level improvement when faced with the challenges of change—especially change in leadership.

A STRONG HIGH SCHOOL JOINS THE CCCII PROJECT

Southern Edge High School (SEHS) is the only high school in a community of approximately 2,900 people. A majority of residents are semiskilled workers or laborers, many employed in the agriculture industry. Several nearby lakes have drawn numerous retirees to the area as "second home" residents. The Southern Edge Independent School District (SEISD) has three other campuses—an elementary school, a middle school, and an alternative high school.

Approximately 450 students, in grades 9–12, are enrolled in SEHS, but enrollment is increasing slowly. SEHS offers a comprehensive curriculum including vocational agriculture and home economics. Participation in extracurricular activities is high, at 96%. The school's racial makeup is 92% white, 4% Hispanic, and 4% African American. Twenty-two percent of the enrolled students are eligible for the free- or reduced-lunch program. SEHS boasts a dropout rate of less than 1%, an average attendance rate of 95.5%, and a state academic performance rating of "exemplary."

Natalie Stewart is the principal of Southern Edge. Stewart's administrative team includes a full-time assistant principal, a full-time counselor, a librarian/technology coordinator, and a department head for each academic program. SEHS instructional staff includes 34 certified teachers and 5 paraprofessionals. About half of the teachers reside within the school district. Seventy percent of the staff have been at SEHS for less than 15 years. All faculty are white and there is gender balance. About one third have master's degrees.

The 2000–2001 school year marked the fourth year that SEHS has operated on a 90-minute block schedule. Block scheduling allows each teacher to have four instructional periods of 90 minutes each day with 45 minutes of team planning and 45 minutes of individual planning. The two principals preceding Stewart were strong advocates of cooperative learning and all of the school's instructional staff received extensive training in cooperative learning strategies for their classrooms. While no whole-faculty in-service on cooperative learning had been held in the previous 3 years, a veteran teacher offered a brief overview to new faculty during their orientation.

Students at Southern Edge take the state test required for graduation during their sophomore year; for the majority of students, that leaves 2 full academic years to learn and grow, free from state-wide tests. The opportunity to participate in SEDL's Creating Communities of Continuous Improvement and Inquiry project was welcomed by the principal and staff at Southern Edge as a means of helping a strong school serve its students more fully. Stewart thought the CCCII project could assist in focusing attention on ways to enrich the students' last 2 years of high school with learning opportunities while helping staff become participants in a professional learning community.

When the SEDL project was initiated, Stanton Weeks had been superintendent for over 10 years and had hired Stewart as the high school principal. When Mr. Weeks was informed of the invitation to participate in the CCCII project, he advised Stewart to pursue it. This mutual respect characterized the working relationship between them.

For example, Stewart was allowed a great deal of freedom in selecting her leadership team. The assistant principal she selected, Holden Cash, initially served only part-time. At the end of his first year as assistant principal, Cash relinquished his coaching responsibilities and became a full-time administrator. While no other officially designated administrative positions exist at SEHS, myriad projects and operations within the school provide individuals and groups with opportunities for leadership.

Of particular importance to the story shared here is Hope Tchrnowski, Librarian/Technology Coordinator at SEHS. SEHS staff adopted the increased integration of technology into the instructional program and into routine procedures at the school as the school-wide CCCII focus. Tchrnowski was exceptionally knowledgeable and skilled in both the equipment and applications of technology. She devoted time and energy beyond her job description to help assure that teachers and students had appropriate technology available and operational. Given her expertise, it was natural that Tchrnowski serve on the school's steering committee for the CCCII project, referred to hereafter as the PLC steering committee.

Stewart, Cash, Tchrnowski, and teacher representatives from math, English, social studies, foreign language, special education services, and science worked with the co-developer in guiding the CCCII project at SEHS. Their willingness to meet and discuss a variety of issues and possible plans for implementing project efforts exemplified the expanding leadership base at the school. The initiative truly became a school-based project as the superintendent empowered the principal to involve the staff, and the principal in turn encouraged staff leadership in deciding how the project might best be implemented. The initial year brought SEHS staff a general understanding of the partnership with SEDL and of professional learning communities in general, identified the school-wide focus as technology, and closed with the anticipation of conducting a site-planned staff development day focused on the current uses of technology throughout the school. But plans for the site-planned staff development day were scrapped as the second year of implementation efforts got underway—things in the district were changing.

THE EFFECTS OF CHANGES AND TRANSITIONS AT SEHS

Dexter Turnan, the new superintendent, was hired at the beginning of the second year of PLC implementation efforts at Southern Edge High School. As Fullan (1999) notes, with the change of superintendent often comes a change of initiatives and a shift in the priorities for the allocation of human and nonhuman resources. Turnan brought "a new way of doing business" to the district. The changes he initiated had numerous intended and unintended consequences that were felt across all aspects of school operations.

Changes in Procedures

At the school, Turnan's new way of doing business caused disruptions in various operations that had become routine. Stewart and her assistants switched their focus to understanding the new procedures and trying to develop a relationship with the new district leader. Instead of focusing on school projects—including the development of a PLC—they turned their attention toward people and issues outside the school, primarily at the district level.

For example, the annual budgeting process for SEHS had functioned internally in a collaborative and cooperative environment between and among the school divisions and departments. Department heads and leaders from each division came together with identified "needs" and "wants" for their individual units for the coming school year. At this meeting, their requests were voiced to the whole group. As general agreement was reached, the cumulative costs of the items were tallied and compared to budgeted funds for the school. Various negotiation strategies helped these school leaders prioritize budget needs and cooperate in securing needed resources—even if it meant other units had to postpone obtaining some of their desired equipment or materials.

This internal process was truly cooperative and demonstrated the way that individual units at the school considered whole-school perspectives in resource allocation decisions. While this internal process for budgeting remained the same at the school after the new superintendent arrived, procedures for the allocation of funds *to* the school from the district office changed. Allocation amounts and procedures for requesting additional funds were not disseminated when expected. As time grew short, the frustration level at the high school increased. Administrators and teacher leaders were anxious to know what funds would be available as they planned for the coming year.

Even after the information arrived and the budgets were developed, the frustration at the high school lingered, leading some to conclude that Turnan didn't understand "what it is like" at the building level. Although the allocation of resources resulted in the high school getting monies, heretofore controlled at the central office, to install a much-needed computer lab, the process was different than previously and the timeline had not aligned with the self-perceived needs of the school staff. The advantage resulting from additional resources was initially overshadowed by negative feelings generated by the arbitrary change in the budgeting process.

A new process was also instituted for spending funds. The previous superintendent, Stanton Weeks, had arrived during a period in which financial concerns were paramount. During his tenure, SEISD had become financially solvent. Mr. Weeks's fiscal management style had been conservative and hands-on. Principals had worked through him and discussed the needs of their schools and the timing of their purchases. They had taken emergency budget issues directly to Superintendent Weeks.

In contrast, Turnan delegated this responsibility to the business clerk. The business clerk had always been involved; however, under the new process, the principals went directly to the business clerk, not through Turnan first. As requests were made and denials and/or approvals resulted, frustration with the process increased at SEHS. Not working directly with the superintendent and often being told no by a staff clerk moved Stewart's reactions from frustration to anger. Having a clerk at the central office empowered to direct her decision-making did not sit well. The issue was not a like or dislike of the central office clerk; rather, Turnan seemed to have delegated the supervision of principals' fiscal management to a noncertified staff position.

After several situations in which Stewart received a no or a significant delay on requested purchases, she expressed her concerns directly to Turnan. In response to Stewart's protests and concerns, Turnan placed himself back in direct contact with the principals on purchasing and budget issues. Unfortunately, Stewart's sense of having been slighted—perhaps even betrayed—in Turnan's earlier delegation of fiscal responsibilities was not so easily remedied.

Another example that directly affected the CCCII project work related to the time for staff development. The previous year, SEHS's PLC steering committee had asked to use one of the staff development days in the fall to share ways in which technology was being used in classroom instruction. Past practice regarding staff development had some days used for district-wide in-services and other days for buildings to address their unique needs. The day selected by the steering committee to share technology uses was one of these building-planned days.

The assistant superintendent called Stewart shortly after the school year started and informed her that plans for that day had changed. Several representatives from the school would be sent to attend a state meeting on grants; others would be required to attend a regional meeting on the new state curriculum initiatives; and some representatives were also needed at a district CPR training. It became obvious that by the time representatives to each of these central office-required meetings were counted, less than half of the faculty would remain in the building that day—certainly less than ideal for sharing particulars about a school-wide initiative on technology use.

Stewart called central office and explained how the project plans had been disrupted by these recent directives from the central office. In response, SEHS was promised an "early release" day later in the year for building-level staff development. As it turned out, this change probably worked better than the original plan. The early release day came in the spring, so that the staff had much more time to actually use some of the new technology installed in the building. When spring came, the experiences to be shared were more varied and in-depth than would have been true in the fall. But this benefit was unforeseen, and the staff's immediate reaction to the change was to feel that, once again, their desires and plans for school improvement had been ignored.

At the end of the school year, another incident further ruptured relationships between SEHS administration and the new superintendent. District finances required some program reductions to stay within available revenues for the coming year. Stewart and her assistant, Cash, were instructed by Turnan to cut the art program. Personnel issues became entwined with this proposed cut, and both issues—cutting the program and cutting the teaching position of the individual in the program—were publicly contested at the board of education meeting where the final decision was to be made.

When the controversy heated up, Stewart and Cash felt that Turnan denied his role in initiating this change. Ultimately, the board supported the personnel termination but maintained the art program as a curricular offering. The controversy, the accusations made in the public forum of the board meeting, and the final recommendations acted on by the board were perceived by Stewart and Cash as another experience of being abandoned by the superintendent. From their perspective, they had done what Turnan had told them to do—namely, eliminated the art program. They felt left on their own to bear the brunt of the emotional public comments that had been offered at the board meeting. Consequently, they lost trust in district leadership.

Not Change, But Transition

In *Managing Transitions* (1991), William Bridges recognizes that the products of change—allocations, procedures, relationships, and so on—are much less objectionable than the process of incorporating the newness. He states: "It isn't the changes that do you in, it's the transitions" (p. 3). He defines "change" as "situational" and "transition" as "the psychological process people go through to come to terms with the new situation" (p. 3). Two points in Bridges's work seem especially appropriate in understanding the SEISD story. First, according to Bridges,

> The starting point for transition is not the outcome but the ending that you will have to make to leave the old situation behind. Situational change hinges

on the new thing, but psychological transition depends on letting go of the old reality and the old identity you had before the change took place. . . . Transition starts with an ending—paradoxical but true. (p. 4)

Second, Bridges asserts: "Before you can begin something new, you have to end what used to be. . . . So beginnings depend on endings. The problem is, people don't like endings" (p. 19).

Whereas Superintendent Turnan might be faulted for having paid too little attention to the way in which his changes would be received, perhaps the greatest fault should be shared: the failure of all parties in the change process to attend to the past, which included expectations, routines, desires, and dreams that had to be acknowledged before they could be released.

Changes in Administrative Relationships

Bridges recommends that change managers accept the reality and importance of the subjective losses, acknowledge the losses openly and sympathetically, expect and accept signs of grieving (denial, anger, bargaining, anxiety, sadness, disorientation, depression), and treat the past with respect. Making clear connections between innovations and the foundations on which they are placed is one way of honoring prior work and accomplishments, and helps to retain a sense of continuous vision and continuing teamwork.

However, there are circumstances that a new manager cannot be expected to recognize, or about which there is little that he or she can do. Superintendent Weeks had brought Natalie Stewart on board as high school principal with an informal agreement of "heir apparent" in place. Stewart served in the district for 2 years in a relationship with the superintendent that was one of mentor/mentee and an unspoken notion that "this will all be yours someday." When Weeks announced his retirement, the board made it clear that Stewart's selection as the new superintendent was not assumed.

Weeks's retirement produced myriad questions: Who would be the replacement? What procedures would be used to identify the replacement? What would the new superintendent's priorities be? Would additional resources be secured? And would the new leadership take some initiative regarding the need for new facilities? Stewart was not the only one whose attention was diverted by these questions. In a meeting with the PLC project steering committee in the fall of 1998, most of the meeting time was used to speculate on similar questions. During this meeting, rumors that the board of education was seeking someone "male and mid-40s" were voiced. Stewart decided not to apply for the job.

Dexter Turnan had been a principal and assistant superintendent prior to coming to the district. Natalie Stewart had served as a middle school principal and a superintendent prior to assuming the high school principalship at SEISD. Understandably upset by the frustration of her expectations, and feeling that she had more experience as a superintendent than did Turnan, Stewart began to criticize Turnan's actions soon after he took the position. The relationship between them developed into one of competition rather than mutual support, and the absence of advocacy pervaded every interaction between the district and the high school. Stewart's welcome to Turnan was less than warm and the negativism between them quickly became apparent to many.

When SEHS earned an exemplary rating on the state accountability measures, Turnan's statements to the staff, the board of education, and the community at large were perceived to be minimal and unenthusiastic. And when all faculty members—but none of the administrative staff—received a letter from the superintendent thanking them for their participation in the CCCII project, Stewart, her assistants, and the SEHS staff felt justified in their feelings that the superintendent was not acknowledging their accomplishments.

As the rift between Dexter Turnan and Natalie Stewart became wider, Turnan realigned and strengthened relationships with the middle school and middle school principal. Turnan's alignment with that principal affected not only the relationship between Stewart and himself, but to some degree the relationship between the two principals as well. This shift in relationships among administrators affected relationships throughout the organization.

Personnel Changes

Three key personnel at the high school were lost at the end of Turnan's first year as superintendent. One was the team leader in the vocational program. Turnan had reallocated some of the funds previously available to this program and further restricted program funding. Later, he announced that this team leader's program component in the vocational area would no longer be offered. The team leader felt Turnan had treated her disrespectfully. Rather than shift positions within a program, she chose to retire.

A chemistry teacher perceived things within the school to be deteriorating from the collaborative, cooperative climate she had so enjoyed when she first began work in the district. From her perspective, little time was being devoted to nurturing staff, and too much time was being spent on power contests between and among administrators. This was an influential member of the PLC steering committee. She felt the CCCII project was what the school needed—desperately. But she also believed it was unlikely that the district's and school's strong focus on collaboration would be restored any time soon, and that she could spend her time and expertise more productively elsewhere.

Hope Tchrnowski also served on the PLC steering committee. She was the Librarian/Technology Coordinator at SEHS and a walking, talking, caring reference on technology. Having once been a classroom teacher at SEHS, she was a well-accepted part of the staff. She had demonstrated her leadership skills in heading up projects, in working closely with administration, and in confronting some tough issues through initiating conversations with the significant players when needed. Her enthusiasm for the PLC project was probably unequaled in the school. Not only did the concept of professional learning communities appeal to her own work style, but the selection of technology use as the school-wide focus fit perfectly with her efforts to help staff become more technologically proficient.

Before the CCCII project was initiated at SEHS, Tchrnowski had informally served as the technology coordinator for the district. She had no such title and was not paid for such responsibility, but she was a major player in writing technology grants, and assuring equipment purchases were compatible with long-range use plans. She even conducted training, either in groups or one-on-one, as needed.

Early in his tenure, Turnan made it clear that he viewed technology as essential to the district if SEISD was to serve its students well. In various meetings he spoke in visionary terms of the need to "leap into technology." Some of his language indicated an in-depth knowledge of technology hardware, software, and possible strategies for embedded technology in classroom instruction. Tchrnowski's excitement at having the PLC project to assist at the building level and a technology-savvy superintendent advocating at the district level was initially high.

Soon, however, it became apparent to Tchrnowski that Turnan's knowledge might not be as in-depth as it first appeared. Probably even more discouraging to her was his unwillingness to work from what already had been done toward technology in the district. Prior to Turnan's arrival, equipment had been purchased, software compatible with that equipment was installed, and wiring and rewiring had been completed. The SEHS staff had lived through these disruptions, and Tchrnowski had held hands, patted heads, and listened to tirades as she went beyond expectations to make all of the equipment usable.

When the new computer lab for SEHS was announced, Tchrnowski was as excited as anyone. The new lab would be available for all classes.

Teachers of any subject area could schedule the lab so their students could work on various projects including writing reports, finding sites on the Internet, and creating multimedia productions. Tchrnowski drew up the specs for the lab equipment and software and reviewed it with Stewart. The purchase request was then sent to central office for approval and purchase. Soon the phone rang; it was Turnan, with questions and suggested changes about the amount and type of equipment as well as the vendors being used.

Tchrnowski explained the needs of the building and compatibility issues between the items being requested and the equipment already in the school. She also cautioned the superintendent about using vendors that had not performed well in the past. Tchrnowski felt that the superintendent listened to her carefully and appreciated her expertise. She was hurt, disappointed, and angered when her recommendations were ignored. Equipment not compatible with existing items was purchased; vendors with whom the district had had poor service in earlier dealings were contracted; and extensive rewiring was necessary to make new equipment work with what was already in place.

As Tchrnowski began to work with the new equipment, her feelings intensified. In her mind, her expertise had been sought; problems she had predicted and fought to avoid were now being given to her to solve. Her initial enthusiasm for the technology-savvy superintendent was gone, and her hopes for being selected as district technology coordinator dimmed.

Tchrnowski's doubts about her future were confirmed when Turnan chose the district's technology coordinator from the middle school. Disappointed that she was not the choice for the position, responsibility, and pay, Tchrnowski nonetheless found herself to be the source of expertise for the new technology coordinator, who called on her for advice and information. After much personal turmoil, Tchrnowski decided to submit her resignation and leave the district.

Every school and district has staff turnover; it's a part of life in any organization. Every organization that experiences change can expect that some staff may leave because they feel uncomfortable with the new direction. Sometimes such departures are both encouraged and celebrated for the boost they give to implementing the new initiatives.

SEHS lost three staff members directly because of the changes in the district initiated by the new superintendent. In a time when the business community was pushing for greater relevance between the school curriculum and post–high school employment, it seemed a net loss for a well-respected vocational program educator to choose to retire rather than participate in the dismantling of a successful cooperative work program with businesses in the community. It was unfortunate to lose a hard-to-staff academic area science teacher because she perceived that a strong cooperative and collaborative culture was losing ground. And, in this time of advocacy for helping youth to become technology literate, it was distressing to lose a highly trained and professionally committed teacher leader in technology because of—and in the midst of—new technology initiatives.

A NEW YEAR

The 2000–2001 school year in Southern Edge Independent School District is well underway as I write this. Vacant positions at the high school have been filled through new hires or reassignments of existing staff. Natalie Stewart and Holden Cash still occupy the two administrative positions at the high school and report that things are off to a great start for the academic year. For now, Stewart and Cash have shifted to an internal focus regarding their work. They acknowledge that there is little or nothing they can do to change things at the district, and have decided that they will focus inward or, as they say it, "inside the bubble" at SEHS.

"Inside the bubble" they can work with the staff, students, and parents of SEHS to continue their exemplary status on state tests, increase the use of technology in enriching instructional practice, and improve their home-school-student partnership by making better use of their various communication mechanisms. They have concluded they will deal with district changes in procedures and personalities as best they can and do it in such a way to minimize any disruptions to the work inside the school.

One meeting of the PLC steering committee has taken place in the current year, and another is scheduled later in the semester. Members of the steering committee who left the school have been replaced with others on the staff. A decision has been to maintain the school-wide focus on technology, but to generate a greater level of involvement by the students. It appears that the efforts to create a PLC at SEHS will continue at the school level, though it will not be soon expanded to include the district context.

At the district level, Dexter Turnan's second year as superintendent has been occupied with the resignation and replacement of a member on SEISD Board of Education, general budget and finance issues, and preparation for a major bond election to generate funds for new facilities.

Perhaps this is where both Turnan and Stewart should have begun—working hard in their separate spheres of influence, concentrating on the positive, and focusing on student needs. During the past year, changes in procedures, relationships, and personnel have resulted in an array of emotions and actions, including anger, distractions, loss of trust, decisions to leave the district, sadness, frustration, and feelings of neglect. Only now are some fences being mended and some new procedures being accepted as simply different, not necessarily bad. While little trust is shared between the district and the high school personnel, there is, at least, less self-absorption in anger, sadness, frustration, and other negative emotions.

Using Bridges's (1991) framework, it seems likely that much of what has occurred and is still occurring in SEISD are attempts by different individuals to manage transitions. According to Bridges, managers need to help members of the organization conclude with the past so that beginnings can commence. Both Turnan and Stewart, as organizational leaders, should have been helping others instead of perpetuating some of the most visible difficulties between themselves—some of Bridges's advice of great relevance, given the happenings of the last year in SEISD.

For example, Stewart needed to give up the ways in which she had interacted with Superintendent Weeks and adopt new ways of interacting with Superintendent Turnan. In order to accomplish this, she most likely would have had to confront and release her aspirations for becoming superintendent herself. Then she might have been able to assist her staff in moving from overidentification with "how we've always done things around here" to a willingness to learn new procedures proposed by Turnan.

In developing procedures, Turnan might have shown a bit more sensitivity, researching earlier methods and considering their continuation. Even if he felt existing procedures should be abandoned, knowledge of them may have assisted him in developing smoother transitions, and would surely have allowed him to appear less autocratic. In a new role and in a new geographic area, Turnan needed to reduce his focus on curriculum and instruction issues and increase his work in the areas of finance, transportation, policy development, and facilities. Perhaps the work of making a transition from assistant superintendent to the superintendent's chief executive role influenced Turnan's actions during this time and reduced his ability to focus on developing relationships and building trust.

As Bridges notes, trust is either mutual or it is shallow. Bennis (1989) also sees trust as a critical issue in leadership. He notes, "I believe that trust is the underlying issue in not only getting people on your side, but having them stay there" (p. 160). Bennis identified four ingredients leaders must have in order to generate and sustain trust:

- *Constancy.* Whatever surprises leaders themselves may face, they don't create any for the group.
- *Congruity.* Leaders walk their talk. In true leaders, there is no gap between the theories they espouse and the life they practice.
- *Reliability.* Leaders are there when it counts; they are ready to support their co-workers in the moments that matter.
- *Integrity.* Leaders honor their commitments and promises. (p. 160)

According to Bennis, "When these four factors are in place, people will be on your side" (1989, p. 160). In the absence of these four factors, as we have seen in the experience of Southern Edge High School, a great deal of professional energy and commitment can be expended to little effect.

IMPLICATIONS

Efforts to create a professional learning community at Southern Edge High School have continued for 2 years. There is willingness on the part of school administration and staff to continue the project. Certainly, there is much still to be done. Could more have been accomplished in the school regarding the creation of a PLC if the difficulties between Turnan and Stewart had not occurred? Probably. But those difficulties did occur—in a school with a strong academic record, with a staff with a rich history of collaboration, with enthusiastic leadership for the project, and with a willing and committed teacher leader facilitating the school's focus on technology.

If this much disruption can occur as a result of district-level changes in a school with the strengths of SEHS, what happens when schools do not have a strong collaborative foundation, when the school itself is the focus of change, or when the continual changes caused by professional turnover in schools derail efforts to make positive change? These questions must be considered by those change agents who would enter schools in difficulty with the goal of total school transformation through development of a professional learning community. As Superintendent Turnan learned, even positive changes can elicit powerful negative reactions.

Superintendents, principals, teachers, staff members, co-developers, and other professionals can all serve as change agents who herald change by their entry into a community and its schools. They may also serve as change managers who seek to assist a community and its school in adapting to change. Both roles require a powerful commitment to an improved future and a great sensitivity to what individuals face as they struggle to release past habits, routines, and treasured hopes.

CHAPTER 13

Building Teacher Leadership Within a Traditional School Structure

Gayle Moller

If professional learning communities provide the best hope for sustained school improvement, and shared leadership is a critical component of successful professional learning communities, then principals must be both willing to share leadership and able to develop conditions and communicate expectations that will advance shared leadership among school professionals.

This chapter focuses on the dimension of supportive and shared leadership and its relationship to emerging teacher leadership. The degree to which school personnel engage in shared leadership can be described along a continuum of supportive and shared leadership indicators, the extremes of which are:

- administrators consistently involve the staff in discussing and making decisions about most school issues while recognizing that there are some legal and fiscal decisions required of the principal; or
- administrators never share information with the staff nor provide opportunities to be involved in decision-making.

In addition, the staff included in decision-making may be: (1) the entire staff; or (2) a small committee, council, or team of staff; or (3) no staff (Hord, Meehan, Orletsky, & Sattes, 1999).

A secondary focus of this chapter is on the PLC dimension of supportive conditions. Examples of actions within this dimension include establishing physical or structural conditions that support the development of a professional learning community. However, Hord (1997a) also included human factors—personal capacities and relationships as well as professional structures—among the aspects comprising the dimension of supportive conditions. In the context of the Creating Communities of Continuous Inquiry and Improvement project, human factors—often the capacity of the principal to share and build leadership—played a particularly important role. These capacities are essential for the success of shared leadership within a professional learning community.

At the start of the CCCII project, none of the 22 participating schools had developed a professional learning community, according to the results of the initial *School Professional Staff as Learning Community* (Hord, 1996) survey and audio-taped interviews (see Chapter 7 for details). However, many schools had, through other efforts, developed some aspects of a PLC at their school, or had structures and practices in place that would assist in the development of a PLC. For example, scheduling practices that afford teachers time to meet together provide the groundwork for the collegiality that a PLC demands. Or a school might have initiated a teacher leadership team by district mandate. The presence of the team implies a greater readiness for a PLC than its absence would. How well the team actually functioned signified whether the school had already developed true shared leadership. Once the teams of coders who evaluated the surveys and interviews identified such markers or characteristics, the markers were used to differentiate between schools judged to be at a "high level of readiness" (HLR) for PLC development, and schools judged to be at a "low level of readiness" (LLR) for PLC development. These markers are listed in Table 13.1.

CHARACTERISTICS OF SCHOOLS AT HIGH AND LOW LEVELS OF READINESS TO DEVELOP PLCs

Understanding how and why school staffs are more or less ready to learn together helps develop our understanding of how principals help or hinder teacher leadership. Four major themes emerged from the survey results: emerging teacher leadership, structural design of shared leadership, the principal's role, and supportive conditions/principal capacities that build shared leadership. These themes are discussed below. The fourth theme—supportive conditions/principal capacities that build shared leadership—is discussed only in terms of HLR schools. Principals at LLR schools often expressed the *value* of these conditions and capacities, but data were evident that these conditions and capacities had not yet been fully implemented and institutionalized.

Emerging Teacher Leadership

Teacher leaders in HLR schools knew they could initiate and facilitate change strategies within their sphere of influence and expertise. These

Table 13.1. Characteristics of HLR and LLR Schools

	High-Level Readiness Schools (HLR)	Low-Level Readiness Schools (LLR)
Emerging Teacher Leadership	Teacher leadership based on expertise	Teacher leadership based on personal stature
	Involved many teachers	Involved a select, elite group of teachers
Structural Design of Shared Leadership	Had structure for shared decision-making	Had structure for shared decision-making
	Fluid structural design changed as needed	Formal design, focused on group process skills
	Longer history of shared decision-making	Relatively new to shared decision-making
Principal's Role	Established trust with principal	Building trust with teachers
	Shared leadership viewed as tool	Shared leadership viewed as obligatory
	Principal is visionary; teachers are leaders	Principal is person in charge
Supportive Conditions	Principal listens	
	Principal knows teacher & learning	
	Principal consistently follows through	

teachers shared a school vision and used their influence to move others toward improved student learning. Although there were formal teacher leaders within these schools, informal teacher leadership also emerged based on expertise. One teacher leader shared the following:

I would almost say that we are a community of leaders. . . . We are a very big school, there are lots and lots of different things that go on. It would be absurd to think that four people could be in charge of everything. . . . What I see the function of the community spirit to be is to identify strengths and divide responsibilities up amongst different members of the faculty . . . defer[ring] to each other for those areas where we might have expertise. . . . It is not unusual, for example, for me to go to the mentor teacher with questions about things concerning new teachers and for her to turn right around and come to me for questions concerning ESL policies . . . since that happens to be my area. And I see that happening all over the staff.

The type of teacher leadership described in the LLR schools was management-oriented and limited to a few teachers. Both teachers and principals in LLR schools described the teacher leaders by their personal characteristics that resulted in being "looked up to," as one principal shared. Descriptions of these teacher leaders include statements such as: "listened to," "present themselves well," "credibility," and "experienced." In these schools there was usually a small elite group of teachers who influenced decisions.

What teachers in schools at different levels of readiness view as important qualities for leadership represents a contrast. While LLR school staffs identify a small group of teachers based on their personal stature among the staff, HLR school staffs seek out teacher leaders for their expertise. Instead of issuing from a select group of teachers, leadership in HLR schools came from a variety of individuals who had expertise in particular areas related to the school's areas of need.

Structural Design of Shared Leadership

Whether recognizing the value of shared leadership or responding to the local mandate to organize in this way, both HLR and LLR schools built structures for shared decision-making. These structures took forms such as leadership teams, school improvement teams, or faculty councils. In some schools the principal selected the teacher members; in other schools the members were elected by a group of teachers they would represent.

The contrasts in the structures were not so much in the procedural decisions as they were in their actual operation. In the HLR schools, the principal and teacher described a fluid, ever-changing arrangement that responded to the immediate needs of the school. Decisions that affected the entire school involved all the staff. In other situations, there were multitiered leadership structures that attempted to put the decision as close as possible to the people who were doing the work. For example, in one HLR school the principal stated, "I have always believed that people closest to decisions that needed to be made should be making them." Believing in this philosophy and putting it into action was not easy for this principal. Leading a recently formed alternative school, she soon realized that members of the new faculty came from traditional school settings and were uncomfortable with participating in a shared decision-making mode. To help the teachers grow in their participation skills, she acknowledged their need for structure in the beginning—she provided them with a meeting schedule and a discussion outline to get started.

Another principal in an HLR school acknowledged the formal structure, but she pulled together informal groups of teachers who were directly affected by a problem, rather than always involving the entire school. The people who were the closest to the action made the just-in-time decisions.

> Let's say that I have looked at data and I have come up with this decision, and I think this is the way to go. . . . So then, I call in my assistant principals, and I say let me go over this with you. What do you think the negatives are to this? What is going to keep us from what we need to do? And they will say, OK, well we maybe need to exchange this, and do that. . . . Then I call in my department chairs and my team leaders. I will say, I have done this and this homework . . . and met with (assistant principals). . . . This is what we have come up with. What do you think? You are the ones that are leading those teams. . . . And then they [give their input] . . . and then I will say, OK, now is everybody together? Nobody is going to walk out of this room and say: "Well, they made us do this."

In the LLR schools, the structure was described as either developing or less developed. Several of the schools' structures were relatively new and they were evolving through the typical group process changes; people were learning how to talk with each other, reach consensus, and determine appropriate decision-making patterns. The development of shared leadership was reflected in statements such as:

- We kind of have shared leadership
- I have begun to share . . .
- It's real new for there to be any teacher leadership. There has been teacher leadership in our building, but not within an organized power structure.

It appeared that the development of shared leadership through decision-making structures in the HLR and LLR schools was influenced by the amount of time the structures had been in place (from 1 to 8 years) and the ability of the principal to be flexible in selecting the decision makers based on the issue at hand.

The Principal's Role

Across schools, the teacher-administrator relationships were frequently referred to in terms of trust and respect. Teachers and administrators in both LLR and HLR schools talked about the importance of these relationships. In the LLR schools there was a sense of building trust; in the HLR schools there appeared to be an established trust.

The principals in the HLR schools reported a different relationship with the teachers in the schools compared to principals in the LLR schools. These principals built on the strengths of the teachers in the HLR schools and played the role of cheerleader and promoter of high expectations that focused on student learning. One principal in an HLR school described how she looked for teacher leadership potential in unlikely places.

> I learned early on, if you don't have the leaders, you create them, you build them, you mold them. You look around. You take that time . . . to see where is the leadership potential. And it wasn't always that vocal person. Although, like in *The Prince* by Machiavelli, you keep the enemies close up. Some of them you give some leading roles to so you can watch them. But you look at the quiet ones. The one who's always doing, always involving the children, always working behind the scenes. That's the person you want to bring up front and they always doubt themselves. So I have to be the greatest cheerleader, the greatest motivator.

The principals in all the schools espoused their beliefs in shared leadership, but the contrast in the two groups of schools was evident in the words the principals used during the interviews. For example, a principal in an LLR school stated: "[I] gave the staff opportunity to select which leadership roles they would like to have." In contrast, a principal from an HLR school said, "I try to develop leadership in every nook and cranny that we have. . . . Everybody does have an opportunity to lead in our school." The principals in LLR schools expressed a desire for teachers to take on leadership roles, whereas the principals in the HLR schools saw it as their responsibility to build the capacity of teachers to take on these roles.

The teacher leaders' language provides insight into the differences between the two groups of schools. A theme from teachers' interviews in LLR schools was that the principal and/or the assistant principals were the "main," "official," "number-one," or "in-charge" leaders in the school. The following statements from teachers in LLR schools show deference to the administration in the school.

- [The principal] is our number-one leader.
- The official leadership is [the principal] and the assistant principal.
- The principal directs the ship.
- The principal would be the first person in charge . . .

Teachers in the HLR schools did not use this type of language. In fact, one teacher leader in an HLR school said: "[The principal] is not necessarily the ultimate leader in the school, but she is the visionary. We are all leaders."

Supportive Conditions/Principal Capacities That Build Shared Leadership

The ability of the principals to provide supportive conditions emerged as a key factor in encouraging shared leadership and nurturing teachers in their new roles. Although principals in the LLR schools spoke of these ideas, it was not evident that they were institutionalized within the school community. The examples shared here are from HLR schools.

Listening. This basic communication skill may be underutilized in most schools, but it is a key tool used by the principals in HLR schools to work with their staffs. Sample statements from teachers and principals include:

- She [the principal] listens.
- [The principal] listens to teachers' complaints as input for action.
- [It is important] to take the time not just to bring in new things, but to talk about how we, organizationally, support each other in this learning process and in making decisions.
- There is a greater recognition (among teachers) that people will listen and try to do something . . . that will make a difference.

Principal Knows About Teaching and Learning. The principals in the HLR schools did not have a "hands-off" approach to curriculum and instruction and other matters related to student learning. They assumed responsibility for knowing what was happening within the school and then became proactive in bringing the right people together to solve the problem. An example of this appears in the following principal's statement:

So then we made lesson plans and I put an assistant principal in each one of their classrooms for the full time. . . . My teachers in

the beginning were like, You are going to be in my classroom? . . .
It only took a couple of times for us to be in there that they realized, yeah, they are not here to criticize, they are here to help. We
had no discipline problems, and we scored 90% and above in
every part of the Writing [standardized test]. Those kids worked
hard and the teachers . . . when we looked at the end they said,
You know, if you had not made us do these a dozen times, and
had not come into our classrooms the way you do, we would not
have reached it. . . . And that is kind of an idea that we had to
cram down but it worked. We did it and the kids are . . . ninety
percent and above in every subject.

Consistent Follow-Through. The HLR school people recognized the
importance of following through on decisions made in the school. Teachers could rely on administrators assuming responsibility for actions they
agreed to take. The following statements from principals and teachers
illustrate this support:

- The principal carries it out.
- It is important [for administration] to keep trying to follow through
  and do what we say we intend to do.
- Talking is one thing—acting is another.

IMPLICATIONS

At the beginning of the second phase of the CCCII, we found a small
number of principals who shared leadership and provided conditions to
support teacher leadership. Within the current hierarchical structure of
schools, these principals appeared to have a high stage of ego development
that was not threatened by the uncertainty of teachers assuming leadership roles. The principals were confident enough in their knowledge of
teaching and learning that they were not reluctant to recognize teacher
expertise in order to build leadership throughout the school. These principals were good listeners. Rather than focusing on the negative factions
in the school, they found those teachers who could lead their colleagues
in positive ways. When teachers and staff members made decisions, the
principal was consistent in following through on those decisions. Their
attention to controlling and monitoring the shared decisions is different
from the need to control all decisions. Teachers were not resentful, but
actually expressed a relief that someone was making sure the decisions
were carried out as they planned.

To expect the thousands of individuals in the principalship to exhibit these high-level skills at all times in their leadership is unrealistic. Principals represent the continuum of human experience. As do other people, they go through life transitions that affect them personally, which, in turn, may influence their leadership. The complex interpersonal relationships between teachers and administrators can result in what may appear to be the principal's callous approach to the concerns of the individual teachers. Protecting one's self-esteem while trying to build the capacity of others can be a daunting task. Personal histories and perspectives enter into the mix and the result can be alienation between the principal and the staff.

External change agents can engage in work with principals with the best of intentions. Principals can eagerly initiate continuous improvement through professional communities. But success beyond the enthusiastic beginnings of any project demands a high level of leadership that recognizes the importance of day-to-day encouragement of a long-term shared vision. Currently, we expect the principal to carry the burden of this work. Ideally, some working structure for shared leadership would exist prior to the development of a professional learning community, which could then be reasonably expected to sustain and advance the quality and breadth of teacher leadership. Otherwise, the implications of this study for establishing professional learning communities—and supporting teacher leadership through PLCs—are not encouraging.

RECOMMENDATIONS FOR PRACTICE

If professional learning communities are supportive of improved student learning and we are working within the existing hierarchical system, then how can we work together to achieve our goals? The following recommendations reflect our learning in this project.

1. Build a structure to support teacher leadership. First, find competent, credible, and approachable teachers who have the needed expertise to act in a leadership capacity. Over time, extend the invitation to other teachers to assume leadership roles. Examine the school day to schedule time for these teachers to work on leadership responsibilities. Principals in HLR schools did not depend on teacher leaders working beyond their normal workday. They covered these teachers' classes, sometimes personally, which gave teachers the time to work together productively. These leaders build school schedules so that teachers who needed to work together would have common planning time.

2. A sense of urgency appears to be a driving force in schools that build teacher leadership for continuous improvement. Find a reason to do the work. Effective principals use data-driven decisions to keep the school working on a shared vision. Once teachers work with data it becomes evident that there are gaps in student learning. Principals who promote teacher leadership collaboratively examine the data with teachers and determine strategies to address the need. The teachers respond to a sense of urgency if the formal leadership facilitates establishing a shared vision based on data. In contrast, one principal of an LLR school posted, with no explanation, student data for individual teachers outside his office door. Although there were no names on the list, the teachers interpreted the message from the principal to mean that they were alone in their struggle to improve student learning.

3. Recruit external change agents who can ask the important questions. These individuals should share the philosophy of the principal so that their work is in tandem rather than at cross-purposes. The time spent on an initial contract between these leaders will prevent misunderstandings as the work progresses. When the principal of an LLR school volunteered to participate, the co-developer assumed the principal wanted to learn with the teachers in developing a professional learning community. After a year into the project, it became clear that the principal did not see her role as a facilitator of the process, whereas the co-developer, frustrated by the principal's passive attention to the teachers' needs, felt the teachers viewed her as a communication tool to persuade the principal to address their issues. This type of conflict can be avoided if both the principal and the external change agent develop a contract regarding their roles in the process.

4. The central office, especially the superintendent, must also be actively supportive of the school leadership's desire to build professional learning communities. Both pressure and support from top-level leadership in the system can help the principal to focus on this important work. Visits to the school, talking to teachers, and listening to progress reports are all strategies that central office leaders can do to help the principal keep the school's actions focused on teaching and learning. A superintendent who participated in the project became an advocate for the schools in his district that were attempting to develop professional learning communities. The principals of these schools knew they had his support, but they also realized that the superintendent held high expectations for them to succeed in the process.

5. Recognize that external change agents can only provide ideas and resources, and serve as a frequent measuring stick for the school's progress. Day-to-day progress and support is the responsibility of the

principal and other leadership *within* the school. If these school leaders are not able to give teachers daily encouragement and expect an external person to make the system work, then the result will be disappointing. Purposeful, ongoing conversations in the hallways, near the mailboxes, and in other informal settings help maintain the focus on improved student learning. A principal of an HLR school knew how to keep the focus on the target by engaging in professional and social interactions with the teachers. She invited teachers to attend relevant conferences with her and during their stay away from home she would arrange for activities where they could have fun together. Not only did this principal keep the conversation alive at school; she used these other opportunities to build trusting relationships supportive of a professional learning community.

CONCLUSION

The complexity of working on the relationships within a school to build leadership capacity can be overwhelming. The principals who appear to be successful in building PLCs do so by expending a high level of energy in their attention to these relationships. The daily attention to the needs of teachers is an obligation that not all principals are able or willing to take on. Senge (1999) suggests that there is a parallel between effective leadership and successful gardening, where the leader must think like a biologist rather than a manager (p. 6). The gardener cannot demand that the plant grow, just like the principal cannot demand that the teacher lead. But we have evidence that principals can work within the complexity of a school to nurture and build the capacity of teachers to be leaders.

The challenge for our profession is to support those talented principals, learn from them, and use this knowledge to help new administrators build their leadership skills. In schools where principals cannot, for whatever reason, relinquish their power to promote positive teacher leadership, the school will be at a disadvantage and the students will not benefit from expanded leadership. These situations present a moral dilemma for both the school system and the community. Can we allow school leaders to inhibit teacher leadership when it results in isolation of efforts and a lack of continuous improvement?

Teaching and Shared Professional Practice—A History of Resistance; A Future Dependent on Its Embrace

Melissa Capers

The preceding chapters explored and documented efforts to instill continuous improvement in schools through creation of professional learning communities (PLC) in schools across the country. As described in Chapter 7, co-developers, trained and supported by SEDL staff, worked in a variety of schools, seeking to assist these schools in improving their teaching effectiveness. The approach they used was intended to improve the means by which the professionals within the school worked together. Specifically, the Creating Communities of Continuous Inquiry and Improvement project focused upon implementing or advancing each of the five dimensions of a professional learning community in each of the participating schools.

THE TEACHING PROFESSION, PROFESSIONAL LEARNING COMMUNITIES, AND SHARED PERSONAL PRACTICE

In the course of the SEDL project, co-developers were often enthusiastically welcomed into schools that took seriously their mission to advance teacher learning in order to increase student learning. Yet, in the most welcoming schools, co-developers confronted some resistance to change. In other schools, the level of distrust, the lack of structural flexibility, debilitating levels of turnover among school and district personnel, lack of resources, and other obstacles combined to make PLC implementation a truly heroic effort.

In most cases, co-developers were able to make progress nonetheless. Co-developers were usually able, at the very least, to help their schools confront and explore the barriers to implementing one or more of the PLC dimensions. This collective consideration provided an opportunity for articulating shared vision and for shared learning. The intellectual exploration of the perceived barriers at a participating school often served as an important first step in developing one or more dimensions of the PLC model.

But despite the enthusiastic embrace of PLC principles in many schools in this study, despite the efforts of co-developers and SEDL staff, and despite various levels of success in each of the other four PLC dimensions, the powerful, multiple, and entrenched barriers to shared personal practice remained virtually unmoved after 3 years of effort. In many of the chapters included in this volume—and at other schools whose stories are not included here—co-developers reported that shared personal practice did not emerge as envisioned. Teachers did not visit one another's classrooms, collaboratively review student work, or engage in significant critical feedback with their colleagues. Their own reluctance to do so rested inside structural barriers including lack of training, lack of time, lack of a culture of collaboration, and lack of leadership support for shared practice.

The struggles and successes of particular schools have been well documented in certain chapters of this volume, and critical aspects of interest and import in the development of PLCs have been illuminated in others. The difficulty of establishing shared personal practice is woven through the narratives, and establishing shared personal practice is often included as part of intended "next steps" in the schools' continued development and improvement. Chapters 5 and 6, which attended to the critical analysis of such issues as leadership and trust, confirmed their impact on the development of shared personal practice in the developing culture of the schools. However our partner schools choose to continue their journeys of development, they will, at some point, encounter the need to develop shared practice. Once implemented, shared practice will serve as both a measure and means of continued development in each of the other dimensions—shared leadership, shared vision and values, supportive structures, and collective learning.

Given the deeply rooted and widely held resistance to implementing shared practice encountered in this study, our consideration of shared practice might be best served through the use of a broad reflective lens. Since observation and audit (central elements of shared practice) are standard to many professions, this epilogue begins with a comparison of teaching to other professions. A number of striking differences emerge. Other professions share historical and cultural roots that teaching does not; other professions enjoy a prestige that teaching does not; and other professions have clear client relationships and nationally recognized rights and responsibilities that teaching does not have.

The differences between teaching and other professions may help to explain why shared personal practice has not already emerged within the education community, and may help to articulate some of the reasons for the resistance this particular professional practice meets among teachers. Most critically, however, this examination serves to remind us all that teaching *is* different from other professions, in ways beyond those usually discussed in the pejorative. For the most part, American teachers work in high-volume, short-term relationships with students. Within these constraints, teachers seek to make significant positive changes that are difficult to measure accurately, while also living up to mandated measurements that may not—and perhaps should not—be directly connected to classroom activities. Teachers undertake—and usually succeed—at work that is quite difficult, and quite important to us all.

However, neither the success of many students and teachers, nor the difficulty of the task, should reduce our enthusiasm to professionalize teaching. The work of too many good teachers is lost because they do not have access to the channels and means to preserve and pass along their insights and experience. The interest of too many who would become good teachers is wasted, as they become discouraged in the face of faceless bureaucracies, and leave a field that does not seem to value or assist them. And the education of too many students is left too vulnerable to chance, its quality and their enthusiasm for learning impacted by arbitrary placements and antiquated practices.

Teaching must be further professionalized—and teachers must be at the forefront of those efforts. Professional learning communities provide the means through which teachers can be enabled and emboldened to develop individually as professionals, and collectively as a profession. Shared personal practice will be an important part of that development, and this final chapter offers a brief consideration of the considerable and consistent data regarding shared personal practice, in order to assert the importance of overcoming the barriers to it. The author hopes that these reflections might serve as prologue to the continued journey of educational improvement, through helping to organize and energize the thinking and efforts of those who would put shared practice into practice in the nation's schools, and in so doing, improve the practice of teaching, the professional lives of teachers, and the learning of our nation's students.

THE TEACHING PROFESSION: PERCEPTIONS AND PRACTICES

On the whole, few Americans will have many dealings with attorneys; most Americans hope to limit their interactions with doctors to annual certifications of their health. But the vast majority of Americans spend thousands of hours over years of their life in the company of teachers. Through the election of local school board officials, citizens have a much more profound and direct impact on the practice of teaching than on the day-to-day work of accountants or stock brokers. Perhaps it is our very familiarity with teaching that allows us to promote and maintain distorted beliefs about the profession and those who practice it. While lawyer jokes may move in and out of vogue in different times and social circles, a great majority of adult Americans can recite the old bromide: "those who can, do; those who can't, teach." Many adults seem to believe it to be true.

Those who do teach are seen in different lights. The more positive light casts teachers as saintly, otherworldly individuals with unique and inborn talents for shaping the minds and hearts of young people. Bumper stickers and T-shirts with slogans like "Teachers touch the future" are one representation of this characterization. The folkloric quantity of stories about teachers who single-handedly changed a person's life are another.

While positive on the surface, this characterization of teachers leads to destructive practices, including a failure to recognize the need for continuing professional development for teachers. If teachers are born and not made, then attempts to train teachers are a waste of time and effort, and attempts to quantify, communicate, and replicate good practice are affronts to this special population.

Teachers are as susceptible as the rest of us to this saintly view of their profession. Those who teach well are tempted to imagine their strengths to be moral as well as professional, and those who struggle as teachers—whether in their first year or throughout their careers—may leave the field or hide their difficulties. They may conclude there is no help for them, and fear that their problem is not a lack of training, but an expression of their personality—"they're just not cut out to be teachers." Struggling teachers might also fear that their professional difficulties will be judged as a moral failing. If those who can't do, teach—then what will those who can't teach, do?

This same national proverb about teaching communicates another belief about teachers—that they are not "real workers." In fact, teachers as a group work as much or more than other American professionals—more than 50 hours per week and on most "vacation" days (National Commission, 1996). In addition, American teachers spend a greater proportion of their work week within classrooms than their international colleagues, regularly teaching more than 1,000 hours per year, while teachers in other countries average 600–800 hours per year (National Commission, 1996). Yet American teachers continue to be contracted to 6-hour workdays and 10-month years—leading to artificially reduced wages, the continued public perception that teachers "have it easy," and ongoing professional frustration for teachers who simply cannot complete their responsibilities during the time they are contracted and paid to do so. A few years ago, teachers in Virginia began "working to the contract" during a labor dispute. The chaos mounted as teachers refused to put in the hours of off-contract time required for them to grade papers, meet with parents, and complete classroom preparation.

The perception remains that teachers do not work very hard, in part because the belief remains that teaching is not very hard work. Many believe that educational improvement will come not by training teachers to teach better, nor by supporting teachers in improving their practice, but by "holding teachers accountable." Indeed, the National Commission on Teaching and America's Future found that "many states and districts have spent more energy trying to . . . prevent poor teaching than trying to prepare top-flight teachers" (1996, p. 14). The current trend toward standardized testing demonstrates a significant way that public perceptions of and policies toward teaching differ from our beliefs about and approaches to other professions. While the human airline pilot serves as the fail-safe to the automatic pilot, standardized testing in schools is offered as the fail-safe to human teachers—somehow more reliable, more fair, and safer than the individuals who walk the halls with students.

In order to gain some insight into why we treat teaching and teachers so differently from how we treat other professions and professionals, it is useful to examine the structural differences between teaching and other professions. The American Federation of Teachers (Robinson, 1985), the Task Force on Teaching as a Profession (Carnegie Forum on Education and the Economy, 1986), and Murphy and Louis (1999) have developed definitions that highlight some consensus as to what a profession is. Based on this general consensus, a profession can be defined by four broad categories: critical self-consciousness, practical expertise, trustful client relationships, and collegial regulation—including shared personal practice. The discussion that follows explores the way that teaching, as it is currently practiced, differs from other professions in each of these four categories.

Critical Self-Consciousness

Professional critical self-consciousness is most obviously expressed in the development and publication of professional standards by members of the profession. Public trust in these standards is expressed as confidence in the judgment of the professional individual or association. Thus, the Bar Association certifies an attorney's qualifications; the attorney so certified is trusted to develop and implement ethical strategy; and the Bar Association is trusted to assure the attorney's continued adherence to those qualifications, as well as continued competence in his or her practice. In most cases, continued professional development is an integral part of maintaining professional certification, and professional associations establish standards for both the quantity and quality of that continued education.

Professional certifying bodies effectively balance local and national effort. In law and medicine, for example, licenses to practice are administered at the state level, and powerful national associations serve to standardize many aspects of practice nationally, as well as to facilitate communication and the movement of individuals between states.

Historically, while other professions developed associations, teachers turned to unions as their organizing structure (Sykes, 1999). While these unions are now evolving to advocate for professional development and standards of school quality (Chase & Gross, 1999), the "professional union" retains a working-class status that associations never had. In addition, these professional unions were late in moving toward standards, and a number of different public policy organizations filled the void in the interim. Overlapping and competing regulatory bodies diminish the impact of the union and impede the development of a national body— union or association—with the power to establish and enforce standards for new and continuing teachers.

According to the National Commission on Teaching and America's Future (1996), less than half of the nation's teacher preparation programs are nationally accredited. State boards of education certify the new teachers who graduate from these programs, and not all of these state boards cooperate with the Interstate New Teacher Assessment and Support Consortium. The standards the state boards promote are themselves weakened by the common practices of allowing teachers to teach out of field, of issuing emergency certification, and of waiving certification requirements that further weaken the role of the state board. According to the National Center for Education Statistics, more than one quarter of all new teachers enter the field without any certification whatsoever (National Commission, 1996, p. 14).

Once in the field, many teachers continue to work without clear standards of quality to guide their practice or to promote continued improvement. National standards for teaching have been developed by yet another organization, the National Board for Professional Teacher Standards (2001). As these standards have developed through an organization separate from the union that represents teachers or the local school boards that hire them, National Board certification requires voluntary participation on the part of individual teachers. These teachers may not always receive support from their principals, colleagues, or school boards for the additional financial and professional responsibility the pursuit of National Board certification requires.

Practical Expertise

In a culture that disdains the "merely" intellectual, a professional might be seen as an intellectual redeemed by craft. While specialized professional knowledge underpins any professional practice, it is the practice—the craft—that garners appreciation. Professional language is filled with physical metaphors: doctors *combat* illness, stockbrokers *build* portfolios, executives *pursue* profits.

The metaphors often used to describe teaching suggest a misunderstanding of the learning process or of teacher's work. Paolo Freire (1970) criticized the "banking" method of teaching, in which students act as banks into which teachers deposit and from which teachers withdraw information. Scheffler imagined teachers' work as the "methodical insertion of ordered facts into the student's mind" (as cited in Smyth, 2000, p. 492). While these metaphors place teachers in positions of comparative power over students, that power is neither skilled nor benign. As a result, individually and as a group, teachers seem unable to define and describe their work in ways that are clear, vivid, and valuable.

The actual devaluation of teaching can be seen in the decline of the role of teachers, even within schools. Between 1950 and 1993, the number of nonteaching staff in schools increased more than 40%, while the proportion of teachers on the professional staff of schools declined from more than 70% to less than 52%. More than 10% of those teachers are "specialists not engaged in classroom teaching" (National Commission, 1996, p. 48). When universities gain prestige through their researchers and not their teachers, and when elementary and secondary schools employ six other professionals for every four teachers (National Commission, 1996), it becomes apparent that teaching is not considered an important practice, even by those who manage the education of millions.

Specialized or advanced knowledge in teaching is "demeaned," according to the National Commission on Teaching and America's Future (1996):

> Novices who enter without preparation are paid at the same levels as those who enter with highly developed skills. Mediocre teachers receive the same rewards as outstanding ones. And unlicensed "teachers" are placed on the same salary schedule as teachers licensed in two or more subjects. (p. 44)

The very skills that teachers gain through hard work within tough classes are rewarded through the promise that those skills will be allowed to atrophy, as teachers with experience and seniority teach lighter loads and "'better' classes" (National Commission, 1996, p. 44). Status accrues to administrators who work farthest from the classroom—a system that clearly wastes enormous teaching talent.

Trustful Client Relationships

Students, parents, future employers, and various supervising and regulatory populations all assert different—and at times competing—expectations for teachers. Teachers are expected to train students in democracy and marketable skills, to control students physically and intellectually, and to publicly and accurately categorize students as more or less deserving of support or opportunity. These expectations make it difficult to identify the client of a teacher, and may prevent each of these client populations from developing a relationship of trust with teachers who must answer to other populations and priorities.

The relationship between student and teacher is markedly different from that between other professionals and clients. Students are required by law to attend school but, for the most part, neither they nor their parents have much choice as to the school or classroom to which they are assigned. Individual students have little redress if their teachers do not perform their work appropriately or well.

The ability for others—parents, future employers, school administrators, government agencies—to enforce their expectations on teachers dampens the possibilities for trustful relationships between students and teachers. In other professional-client relationships, the clear and primary duty of the professional is to protect the best interest of the client, even when the "common good" may be at stake. Thus, a medical patient's right to privacy is upheld in the case of HIV infection, despite the potential danger to others. Similarly, a defendant's right against self-incrimination is upheld, despite the possibility that such incrimination might help to convict a criminal. Students enjoy no such privilege or protection in their relationship with teachers. In fact, the National Commission (1996) asserts: "On some unconscious level schools tolerate student failure because they mistake it for commitment to high standards" (p. 44). Making a record of a student's inability to successfully demonstrate mastery at the time such demonstration is required is not in the best interest of the individual student, although it may serve the purposes of the school or teacher.

It would be inconceivable for a flight instructor to send all her students up to solo on schedule, regardless of her assessment as to whether a particular student could succeed at flying a plane alone. Yet the government requires more and more standardized testing. These tests are administered on the basis of the calendar, not the student's readiness. They assume—and, in fact, guarantee—that a proportion of students taking the test will fail. In the face of the discouragement, stigma, and lost opportunity such failure can cause, it seems remarkable that any trust whatsoever is retained between students and teachers.

Collegial Regulation

The professional characteristic of collegial regulation most closely approaches shared personal practice. Given the resistance to shared personal practice that was encountered in the CCCII project, it should not be surprising to discover that collegial regulation is all but absent from the teaching profession. While all four of the categories of professionalism are intertwined, perhaps collegial regulation most clearly affects, or is affected by, the others. The weaknesses in the professional practice of teaching, across the categories of critical self-consciousness, practical expertise, and trustful client relationships, converge within the category of collegial regulation. An examination of the intersection of this category with the others demonstrates how particularly debilitating the absence of collegial regulation is to the advancement of the profession and improvement of the practice of teaching.

Collegial Regulation and Critical Self-Consciousness. The professional associations, which support other professions in articulating, communicating, and enforcing standards that arise through critical self-consciousness, also provide the means through which professionals are accessible and accountable to one another for collegial regulation. In the absence of strong, centralized professional associations, teachers have become accountable to administrators, school boards, parents, state departments of education, and others.

Collegial Regulation and Practical Expertise. Teachers are doubly disadvantaged as they face a bevy of regulators while working in extended isolation from their peers. Access to peers is critical to collegial regulation, because collegial regulation requires the articulation of expected expertise. In the absence of these peer relationships, teachers can lose confidence in their own professional expertise, and come to distrust or devalue peer review as, alternately, "one more set of judges" or "just another teacher." Good faith efforts to establish collegial regulation—and thus articulate professional expertise—can also be stymied by the continued need to meet other regulatory requirements that have little relevance to the improvement of teaching practice.

Collegial Regulation and Trustful Client Relationships. Peer relationships can provide professionals the ballast necessary to successfully negotiate multiple relationships and demands. One of the most widely recognized roles of professional organizations is the development of ethical standards for a profession. These standards can then be communicated to professionals through collegial regulation. When communicated to clients, these standards will serve to establish reasonable client expectations and increased trust in teachers as professionals.

STANDARDS-BASED INSTRUCTIONAL IMPROVEMENT AND PROFESSIONAL LEARNING COMMUNITIES

It is very unlikely that any single national association will soon be adopted as the sole arbiter of professionalism in teaching. Given the localized structure of education in the United States, ideally school-based professional communities should be among the first bodies to address the gaps articulated in the previous discussion. Once established, these communities will likely reach out to others in the district, region, and elsewhere— eventually meeting the need for developing national associations and building an effective web of professional services and standards for our nation's teachers. Proponents of a standards-based national education reform look forward to this intersection of efforts by including professional learning communities (or the characteristics of PLC as identified by Hord, 1997a), implicitly or explicitly, in their recommendations:

- The National Board for Professional Teacher Standards includes in their "Five Propositions of Accomplished Teaching" (2001), that "Teachers are members of learning communities."
- Richard Elmore (2000) focuses on shared leadership as an important prerequisite to standards-based reform.
- Among the five recommendations set forth by the National Commission on Teaching and America's Future (1996) are: "reinvent . . . professional development," "encourage and support teacher knowledge and skills," and "create schools that are organized for student and teacher success."

A study comparing high-achieving and low-achieving schools found that 90% of the variation in student achievement in mathematics and reading could be traced to teacher qualifications (National Commission, 1996); another study found that recruiting and developing more highly qualified teachers is the most cost-effective means of improving student achievement (National Commission, 1996). Researchers are in nearly unanimous agreement that real school reform and improvement will come only through the development, transmission, and maintenance of standards of excellence in instructional practice. Nearly all standards-based reform plans call for the development of teacher leadership and involvement that is at the heart of professional learning communities. Why?

Professional learning communities can provide the ground on which standards are observed and developed, the means by which they are conveyed, and the structures through which they are enforced on a school-by-school basis. Teachers must share, identify, articulate, and communicate—to themselves, to each other, and to the public at large—the practices and procedures that facilitate learning and characterize excellent instruction. Unless teachers do this, destructive myths about teachers and teaching will continue to support top-down, one-size-fits-all, add-on, and ultimately failing efforts at school reform.

As researchers continue to call for—and jurisdictions begin to implement—teacher preparation that includes substantial opportunities for internship, residency, or mentoring under the supervision of experienced teachers (National Commission, 1996; Gratch, 2000), peer supervision, observation, and review will become more normalized within schools. Teachers themselves must articulate the hard work and value of teaching. They will gain the perspective, knowledge, skills, and courage to do so through professional learning communities that provide them with supportive leadership and conditions, effective professional development, strong relationships with colleagues, and—yes—the opportunity to welcome and be welcomed as observers and critical friends in classrooms across the country.

A look at how shared practice has affected other professions allows us to look forward to dramatic results from the implementation of shared practice at our nation's schools. In 1993, heart surgeons in Maine, New Hampshire, and Vermont began to observe one another regularly in the operating room and to share insights and approaches with one another on a regular basis. In 2 years, the death rate among their patients fell 25% (Cushman, 1996). We cannot yet know precisely how this level of improvement will show itself in schools, nor whether improvement on quite this scale is possible. But results like these among New England heart surgeons certainly suggest that we have much to look forward to.

Professional learning communities develop fertile ground on which to build shared practice in schools. While the interplay between the PLC dimensions may vary from school to school, it seems clear that, in most cases, shared leadership will precede the other dimensions, and shared practice will be the last to develop. In Chapter 5, Fleming and Thompson pointed out the importance of trust in the development of professional learning communities; trust is both necessary for and flows out of the PLC dimensions, but seems most critical to the implementation of shared practice.

Our CCCII experience has shown us that 3 years is not long enough to develop professional learning communities, though we believe we succeeded in seeding them in many partner schools. Professional learning communities should be self-sustaining; we trust they will be self-generating in schools that have begun this journey with us. In particular, we've found that the road to shared practice is longer than we knew when we began this journey—but we believe it is still the right road to travel.

References

Astuto, T. A., Clark, D. L., Read, A-M., McGree, K., & Fernandez, L. deK. P. (1993). *Challenges to dominant assumptions controlling educational reform.* Andover, MA: Regional Laboratory for the Educational Improvement of the Northeast and Islands.

Barth, R. S. (1990). *Improving schools from within.* San Francisco: Jossey-Bass.

Bennis, W. (1989). *On becoming a leader.* Reading, MA: Addison-Wesley.

Blumberg, A., & Greenfield, W. (1980). *The effective principal.* Boston: Allyn & Bacon.

Bower, M. (1966). *Will to manage.* New York: McGraw-Hill.

Boyd, V. (1992). *School context: Bridge or barrier to change?* Austin, TX: Southwest Educational Development Laboratory.

Boyd, V., & Hord, S. M. (1994a, April). *Principals and the new paradigm: Schools as learning communities.* Paper presented at the annual meeting of the American Educational Research Association, New Orleans.

Boyd, V., & Hord, S. M. (1994b). Schools as learning communities. *Issues . . . about Change, 4*(1). Austin, TX: Southwest Educational Development Laboratory.

Brandt, R. (1995). On restructuring schools: A conversation with Fred Newmann. *Educational Leadership, 53*(3), 70–73.

Brandt, R. (1996). On a new direction for teacher evaluation: A conversation with Tom McGreal. *Educational Leadership, 53*(6), 30–33.

Bridges, W. (1991). *Managing transitions: Making the most of change.* Reading, MA: Addison-Wesley.

Bryk, A. S., & Schneider, B. (1996). *Social trust: A moral resource for school improvement.* Chicago: University of Chicago, Center for School Improvement.

Carmichael, L. (1982). Leaders as learners: A possible dream. *Educational Leadership, 40*(1), 58–59.

Carnegie Forum on Education and the Economy. (1986). *A nation prepared: Teachers for the 21st century.* Washington, DC: The Forum.

Cavanagh, R. F., & Dellar, G. B. (1997, April). *School culture: A quantitative perspective on a subjective phenomenon.* Paper presented at the annual meeting of the American Educational Research Association, Chicago.

Chase, B., & Gross, M. L. (1999, November 15). Q: Are America's teachers well-qualified to teach our children? *Washington, 15*(42), 40–43.

Cuban, L. (1990). Reforming again, again, and again. *Educational Researcher, 19*(1), 3–13.

Cushman, K. (1996, November). Looking collaboratively at student work: An essential toolkit. *Horace, 13*(2), 1–12.

Danielson, C. (1996). *Enhancing professional practice: A framework for teaching*. Alexandria, VA: Association for Supervision and Curriculum Development.

Darling-Hammond, L. (1994). *The current status of teaching and teacher development in the United States*. New York: Teachers College, Columbia University.

Darling-Hammond, L. (1995). Policy for restructuring. In A. Lieberman (Ed.), *The work of restructuring schools: Building from the ground up* (pp. 157–175). New York: Teachers College Press.

Darling-Hammond, L. (1996). The quiet revolution: Rethinking teacher development. *Educational Leadership, 53*(6), 4–10.

Deal, T. E. (1992). Leadership in a world of change. In S. D. Thompson (Ed.), *School leadership: A blueprint for change* (pp. 1–7). Newbury Park, CA: Corwin Press.

Deal, T. E., & Kennedy, A. A. (1982). *Corporate cultures: The rites and rituals of corporate life*. Reading, MA: Addison-Wesley.

Deal, T., & Peterson, K. D. (1990). *The principal's role in shaping school culture*. Washington, DC: U.S. Department of Education.

Edwards, J., Butler, J., Hill, B., & Russell, S. (1997). *People rules for rocket scientists*. Samford, Australia: Samford Research Associates Pty. Ltd.

Elmore, R. F. (2000). *Building a new structure for school leadership*. Boston: The Albert Shanker Institute.

Fleming, G. (1999). Principals and teachers: Continuous learners. *Issues . . . About Change, 7*(2). Austin, TX: Southwest Educational Development Laboratory.

Freire, P. (1970). The "banking" concept of education. In D. Bartholomae & A. Petrosky (Eds.), *Ways of reading: An anthology for writers* (5th ed.). Boston: Bedford/St. Martins.

Fullan, M. (1999). *Change forces: The sequel*. Philadelphia, PA: Falmer Press, Taylor & Francis, Inc.

Fullan, M. G., with Stiegelbauer, S. (1991). *The new meaning of educational change* (2nd ed.). New York: Teachers College Press.

Garmston, R., & Wellman, B. (1995). Adaptive schools in a quantum universe. *Educational Leadership, 52*(7), 6–12.

Garmston, R. J., & Wellman, B. M. (1999). *The adaptive school: A sourcebook for developing collaborative groups*. Norwood, MA: Christopher-Gordon.

Gibbs, J. (1995). *Tribes: A new way of learning and being together*. Sausalito, CA: CenterSource Systems.

Gratch, A. (2000). Teacher voice, teacher education, teaching professionals. *The High School Journal, 83*(3), 43ff.

Hargreaves, A. (1995, April). Renewal in the age of paradox. *Educational Leadership, 52*(7), 14–19.

Hill, F., Lofton, G., & Chauvin, S. (1995, April). *Establishing a collaborative climate: Perceptions of a first year principal and faculty*. Paper presented at the annual meeting of the American Educational Research Association, San Francisco.

Hord, S. M. (1996). *School professional staff as learning community* [Questionnaire]. Austin, TX: Southwest Educational Development Laboratory.

Hord, S. M. (1997a). *Professional learning communities: Communities of continuous inquiry and improvement*. Austin, TX: Southwest Educational Development Laboratory.

Hord, S. M. (1997b). Professional learning communities: What are they and why are they important? *Issues . . . about Change, 6*(1). Austin, TX: Southwest Educational Development Laboratory.

Hord, S. M., Meehan, M. L., Orletsky, S., & Sattes, B. (1999). Assessing a school staff as a community of professional learners. *Issues . . . about Change, 7*(1). Austin, TX: Southwest Educational Development Laboratory.

Kleine-Kracht, P. A. (1993). The principal in a community of learning. *Journal of School Leadership, 3*(4), 391–399.

Kotter, J. (1991). *A force for change*. New York: Free Press.

Kouzes, J. M., & Posner, B. Z. (1990). *The leadership challenge: How to get extraordinary things done in organizations*. San Francisco: Jossey-Bass.

Lee, V. E., Smith, J. B., & Croninger, R. G. (1995, Fall). Another look at high school restructuring. *Issues in restructuring schools*. Madison, WI: Center on Organization and Restructuring of Schools, School of Education, University of Wisconsin-Madison.

Leithwood, K., Leonard, L., & Sharratt, L. (1997). *Conditions fostering organizational learning in schools*. Paper presented at the annual meeting of the International Congress on School Effectiveness and Improvement, Memphis, TN.

Lortie, D. (1975). *School teacher: A sociological study*. Chicago: University of Chicago Press.

Louis, K. S., & Kruse, S. D. (1995). *Professionalism and community: Perspectives on reforming urban schools*. Thousand Oaks, CA: Corwin Press.

McLaughlin, M. W., & Talbert, J. E. (1993). *Contexts that matter for teaching and learning*. Stanford, CA: Center for Research on the Context of Secondary School Teaching, Stanford University.

Midgley, C., & Wood, S. (1993, November). Beyond site-based management: Empowering teachers to reform schools. *Phi Delta Kappan, 75*(3), 245–252.

Morrissey, M. S. (2000). *Professional learning communities: An ongoing exploration*. Austin, TX: Southwest Educational Development Laboratory.

Murphy, J., & Louis, K. S. (Ed.). (1999). *Handbook of Research on Educational Administration* (2nd ed.). San Francisco: Jossey-Bass.

National Board for Professional Teaching Standards. [Home Page of the National Board for Professional Teaching Standards], [On-line]. (2001). Available at http://www.nbpts.org. (Accessed January 29, 2001)

National Commission on Teaching and America's Future. (1996, September). *What matters most: Teaching for America's future*. New York: Author.

Newmann, F. M., & Wehlage, G. G. (1995). *Successful school restructuring: A report to the public and educators*. Madison, WI: Center on Organization and Restructuring of Schools, Wisconsin Center for Education Research, University of Wisconsin.

Reiss, F., & Hoy, W. K. (1998). Faculty loyalty: An important but neglected concept in the study of schools. *Journal of School Leadership, 8*, 4–25.

Riedlinger, B. (1998). *The creation and implementation of a school site governance council: Moving toward schools and communities of inquiry.* Unpublished doctoral dissertation, University of New Orleans.

Robinson, V. (1985). *Making do in the classroom: A report on the misassignment of teachers.* Washington, DC: Council for Basic Education, American Federation of Teachers.

Rosenholtz, S. (1989). *Teacher's workplace: The social organization of schools.* New York: Longman.

Sarason, S. B. (1971). *The culture of the school and the problem of change.* Boston: Allyn & Bacon.

Schein, E. H. (1985). *Organizational culture and leadership.* San Francisco: Jossey-Bass.

Scribner, J. D., & Reyes, P. (1999). *Creating learning communities for high-performing Hispanic students: A conceptual framework.* In P. Reyes, J. D. Scribner, & A. Scribner (Eds.), *Lessons from high-performing Hispanic schools: Creating learning communities* (pp. 188–210). New York: Teachers College Press.

Senge, P. (1990). *The fifth discipline: The art and practice of the learning organization.* New York: Currency Doubleday.

Senge, P. (1999). *The dance of change: The challenges of sustaining momentum in learning organizations.* New York: Currency/Doubleday.

Senge, P., Kleiner, A., Roberts, C., Ross, R., & Smith, B. (1994). *The fifth discipline fieldbook.* New York: Doubleday.

Sergiovanni, T. J. (1994). *Building community in schools.* San Francisco: Jossey-Bass.

Smylie, M. A., & Hart, A. W. (1999). *School leadership for teacher learning and change: A human and social capital development perspective.* In J. Murphy & K. S. Louis (Eds.), *Handbook of research of educational administration* (2nd ed.). San Francisco: Jossey-Bass.

Smyth, J. (2000, May). Reclaiming social capital through critical teaching. *The Elementary School Journal, 100*(5) 491–511.

Southwest Educational Development Laboratory. (1998). [How schools develop professional learning communities]. Unpublished raw data.

Sykes, G. (1999). Teacher and student learning: Strengthening their connection. In L. Darling-Hammond and G. Sykes (Eds.), *Teaching as the learning profession* (pp. 151–180). San Francisco: Jossey-Bass.

Wignall, R. (1992, June). *Building a collaborative school culture: A case study of one woman in the principalship.* Paper presented at the European Conference on Educational Research, Enschede, The Netherlands.

Zemelman, S., Daniels, H., & Hyde, A. (1998). *Best practice: New standards for teaching and learning in America's schools.* Portsmouth, NH: Heinemann.

About the Authors

Shirley M. Hord is Scholar Emerita at the Southwest Educational Development Laboratory (SEDL) in Austin, Texas, where she led the day-to-day activities and long-term planning for three projects comprising the Strategies for Increasing School Success Program, all of which focused on educational improvement and increased learning success for students. She continues to monitor and support the Leadership for Change networks and the Concerns-Based Adoption Model (CBAM) constituencies, and designs and delivers professional development that nurtures school leadership and advances school change. Her current professional passion is the creation and implementation of professional learning communities in schools and districts.

Dr. Hord holds a Ph.D. in Educational Administration from the University of Texas at Austin. She is the author or co-author of several books, including *Change in Schools: Facilitating the Process* and *Implementing Change: Patterns, Principles, and Potholes.* Dr. Hord may be reached at SEDL, 211 E. Seventh St., Austin, TX 78701 or by email: *shord@sedl.org.*

D'Ette Cowan is a program associate at the Southwest Educational Development Laboratory (SEDL) in Austin, Texas, where she develops, implements, and reports on successful approaches to systemic educational reform. In her work at SEDL, she provides direct assistance to districts and schools with high populations of economically disadvantaged students. She is a certified teacher, reading specialist, and principal, and has taught reading at the middle school level and served as an elementary school principal. She received her Ed.D. in educational administration from the Public School Executive Leadership Program at the University of Texas at Austin in 2001. She has authored and co-authored numerous reports and papers on principal leadership, professional learning communities, comprehensive school improvement, and systemic reform.

You may reach Dr. Cowan at SEDL, 211 E. Seventh Street, Austin, TX 78701 or by email: *dcowan@sedl.org.*

Grace L. Fleming maintains a personal mission to reduce poverty and other social ills by delivering effective education resources to low-income populations. She joined the Southwest Educational Development Laboratory (SEDL) to bring 10 years of experience in developing programs for low-income populations to school improvement initiatives. Her work at SEDL included guiding schools to develop partnerships with families and communities and establishing professional learning communities as part of the Strategies for Increasing School Success. Since leaving SEDL, Ms. Fleming continues her mission to limit the spread of poverty by focusing on adults seeking higher education to improve their job market-ability. She holds a B.A. in Spanish and an M.A. in Sociology.

Tara Leo Thompson is a program specialist at the Southwest Educational Development Laboratory in Austin, Texas. Ms. Thompson works with school districts in SEDL's five-state region to enable districts to become high-performing learning communities. Ms. Thompson's past work at SEDL has included assisting in the creation and support of professional learning communities and in the development and testing of models, strategies, and tools to support comprehensive reform.

Prior to joining SEDL in 1998, Ms. Thompson managed the drop-out prevention program for Communities In Schools–Central Texas, where she developed and implemented direct social services and academic enrichment programs to high-risk students and their parents. She also worked closely with school staff in implementing individual student plans to ensure student success.

Ms. Thompson holds a B.A. in Psychology and an M.S. in Social Work from the University of Texas at Austin. You may reach her at SEDL, 211 E. Seventh Street, Austin, TX 78701 or by email: *tleo@sedl.org*.

Melanie S. Morrissey joined the Southwest Educational Development Laboratory (SEDL) staff in 1998 after teaching for 9 years at the elementary level. At SEDL, she spent several years researching the development of professional learning communities within school systems. Applying the research in her work with staff at low-performing schools, Ms. Morrissey found that the development of professional learning communities supported staff and students by improving teaching and learning conditions, and provided the necessary foundation for making progress toward their improvement goals. She continues to work with schools to develop professional learning communities as a structure for continuous improvement. Ms. Morrissey holds a master's degree in Special Education and is the author of *Professional Learning Communities: An Ongoing Exploration.* You may reach Ms. Morrissey at SEDL, 211 E. Seventh St., Austin, TX 78701 or by email: *mmorriss@sedl.org*.

Anita Pankake, a former teacher, team leader, assistant principal, and principal, is currently a professor in the Department of Educational Leadership at the University of Texas–Pan American in Edinburg, Texas. Dr. Pankake holds undergraduate and master's degrees from Indiana State University–Terre Haute, and a doctorate from Loyola University.

Dr. Pankake has published in the *Journal of Staff Development, Educational Considerations, NASSP Bulletin, Journal of School Leadership, Journal of Instructional Psychology,* and other professional journals and has served as the managing editor of the *Catalyst for Change* journal for ten years. She is the author of two books—*The Effective Elementary School Principal* and *Implementation: Making Things Happen*—and is the co-editor of two books. *Implementation: Making Things Happen* was named the Outstanding Publication for the Year 2000 by the Texas Staff Development Council. Recently Dr. Pankake was honored to be named by the National Staff Development Council as co-editor with Dr. Jody Westbrook-Youngblood for the *Journal of Research in Professional Learning,* a new online, peer-reviewed journal. She is an active member of several national and state professional associations including Association for Supervision and Curriculum Development, National Staff Development Council, Texas Staff Development Council, Texas Council of Women School Executives, and Texas Association for Supervision and Curriculum Development.

Kristine Kiefer Hipp is an associate professor in the College of Education at Cardinal Stritch University, Milwaukee, Wisconsin. She teaches in a master's program in Educational Leadership and a doctoral program in Leadership for the Advancement of Learning and Service, a non-traditional program that focuses on personal, organizational, and social transformation. Dr. Hipp consults widely, facilitating organizational change in K–12 schools/districts related to her research in leadership, professional learning communities, and collective efficacy. She has presented her research at the local, state, national, and international levels, and has published articles in national and international journals and book chapters. Currently, Dr. Hipp is co-authoring a book entitled *Reculturing Schools as Professional Learning Communities.*

Prior to her work at Cardinal Stritch University, Dr. Hipp taught in a master's program in Educational Leadership at Ball State University in Muncie, Indiana. She worked for the School District of Janesville for 25 years as a special education teacher/support teacher, district-level staff developer, graduate-level adjunct at the University of Wisconsin–Whitewater, a consultant in effective teaching practices, and a research assistant at the University of Wisconsin–Madison where she earned her Ph.D. in Educational Administration. Contact Dr. Hipp at *kahipp@stritch. edu* or (414)410-4346.

Jane Bumpers Huffman, associate professor of Educational Administration, teaches graduate courses at the University of North Texas. Her areas of interest include change management, leadership, professional development, and learning communities.

Dr. Huffman is the program coordinator for, and has directed, the annual Assistant Principals' Conference for six years. She worked in the Norman, Oklahoma public schools for 10 years as a teacher, school administrator, and staff development administrator. Dr. Huffman also served as a research assistant at Southwest Educational Development Laboratory in Austin, Texas. She has published twelve articles, five book chapters, and is a co-author of a forthcoming book entitled *Reculturing Schools as Professional Learning Communities*. Contact Dr. Huffman at *huffman@unt. edu* or (940)565-2832.

Richela Chapman has worked in the field of education for 29 years, as a teacher and then as a specialist and facilitator at one of Texas's Regional Education Service Centers. One of the highlights of her career occurred in 1997 when she was selected to participate in SEDL's Creating Communities of Continuous Inquiry and Improvement project. Through this project, she selected a small, rural school to guide in becoming a professional learning community and improving student achievement.

While at the Region XVI Education Service Center, Ms. Chapman worked in various capacities: Gifted/Talented Specialist, Curriculum and Staff Development Specialist, Partnership Schools Facilitator, and Title I/State Compensatory Education Specialist. She provided management and leadership training and technical assistance to improve student performance, as well as directed school improvement and accountability teams. Her education career began as a substitute teacher and classroom aide. She served as a classroom teacher for 12 years prior to joining the education service center.

Ms. Chapman holds an M.A. in Special Education/Gifted from California State University, Los Angeles, where she had the honor of studying with internationally recognized professor Dr. Barbara Clark. She earned a bachelor's degree in elementary education and mid-management certifications from West Texas A&M University in Canyon, Texas.

Dawn Watson graduated from Texas Tech University in 1991 with a Bachelor of Science degree in Home Economics Education. After graduating from Texas Tech, she taught Home Economics for 3 years at Loop, Texas. Upon leaving Loop, she opened an alternative high school where she was principal for 2 years. During this time she received her Masters of Education from Sul Ross University.

Watson left the alternative school and was a high school principal for a year before accepting a principal's position at the elementary school where she became involved in the Southwest Educational Development Laboratory's Creating Communities of Continuous Inquiry and Improvement research project.

Watson is currently a Family Consumer Science Extension Agent for the Texas Cooperative Extension in Donley County.

Brian Riedlinger is President and CEO of the School Leadership Center of Greater New Orleans, a privately funded project in association with Baptist Community Ministries (a private foundation), the University of New Orleans, and Xavier University. Previously, he was a principal for 20 years at the elementary and junior high school levels in New Orleans.

Recognition of Dr. Riedlinger's school leadership work includes acknowledgment by the *New York Times* as one of ten effective schools nationwide, and the National Endowment for the Arts as one of sixteen schools with outstanding arts programs nationwide. Dr. Riedlinger was also honored as Louisiana State Principal of the Year. Currently, his work at the Center focuses on school improvement, with particular attention to school leadership and the principal's role in increased student achievement. Dr. Riedlinger also teaches at the University of New Orleans and consults nationally on leadership training.

Dianne F. Olivier is the Director of Curriculum and Instruction for St. Martin Parish School System, Louisiana. She holds bachelor's and master's degrees in education and an Educational Specialist degree in administration and supervision from the University of Southwestern Louisiana. She received a Ph.D. from Louisiana State University in Educational Leadership and Administration, with a minor in Psychology.

Dr. Olivier has more than 30 years of experience in public school education, with over 20 years in administration. She is an adjunct faculty member at Louisiana State University. Her research interests are school culture, teacher self and collective efficacy, and professional learning communities.

Gayle Moller is an assistant professor in the Department of Educational Leadership and Foundations in the College of Education and Allied Professions at Western Carolina University in Cullowhee, North Carolina. She was formerly executive director of the South Florida Center for Educational Leaders. The Center served large, urban school districts in South Florida and provided staff development for school leaders who were striving to improve schools.

Dr. Moller worked in the Broward County Public Schools (Ft. Lauderdale, Florida) for 19 years as a teacher, school administrator, and staff development administrator. She has designed professional development programs for teachers since 1971. For 6 years, she developed and carried out an extensive leadership development program within the Broward County Public School system.

Dr. Moller received her doctorate from Teachers College, Columbia University. Her graduate work centered on staff development for shared decision-making. She is a co-author of the book *Awakening the Sleeping*

Giant: Helping Teachers Develop as Leaders, 2nd Edition. Dr. Moller also served on the Board of Trustees of the National Staff Development Council.

Melissa Capers holds an M.F.A. in Fiction Writing and an M.A. in Composition and Rhetoric from Virginia Commonwealth University. Prior to working with Southwest Educational Development Laboratory on the Creating Communities of Continuous Inquiry and Improvement project, Melissa taught college composition in Virginia and Texas, and worked at the Virginia Department of Education's Division of Homeless Children's Services. Ms. Capers is currently living in Northern Virginia and working as a freelance writer. This work allows her to pay the bills and to keep learning about subjects as wide-ranging as organ transplant technology and bioterrorism preparedness. Freelancing has also provided her the time to complete a novel, to teach creative writing at The Writers Center in Bethesda, MD, and to start an earnest search for a literary agent. Her short stories and essays have appeared in *Western Humanities Review*, *Louisville Review, Pearl, The Sun*, and others

Index